# Saddle Up, New Mexico!

## The Statewide Horse Trail and Travel Guide

Text and photography by

**John and Nina Buonaiuto-Cloyed**

**WESTCLIFFE PUBLISHERS**

westcliffepublishers.com

**ISBN-10:** 1-56579-535-0
**ISBN-13:** 978-1-56579-535-8

**TEXT & PHOTOGRAPHY COPYRIGHT:** John and Nina Buonaiuto-Cloyed, 2006. All rights reserved
**MAPS COPYRIGHT:** F + P Graphic Design, Inc., 2006. All rights reserved.

**EDITOR:** Jennifer Jahner
**DESIGN:** Rebecca Finkel, F + P Graphic Design, Inc.
**PRODUCTION MANAGER:** Craig Keyzer

**PUBLISHED BY:** Westcliffe Publishers, Inc.
P.O. Box 1261
Englewood, Colorado 80150
westcliffepublishers.com

**PRINTED IN CHINA BY:** C & C Offset Printing Co., Ltd.

**LIBRARY OF CONGRESS CATALOGING-IN-PUBLICATION DATA:**

Buonaiuto-Cloyed, John.
Saddle up, New Mexico! : the statewide horse trail and travel guide /
text and photography by John and Nina Buonaiuto-Cloyed.
p. cm.
Includes index.
ISBN-13: 978-1-56579-535-8
ISBN-10: 1-56579-535-0
1. Trail riding—New Mexico—Guidebooks. 2. Trails—New Mexico—
Guidebooks. 3. Forest reserves—New Mexico—Guidebooks 4. New
Mexico—Guidebooks
I. Buonaiuto-Cloyed, Nina. II. Title.
SF309.256.N6C56   2006
798.2'309789—dc22

                                        2006015243

*For more information
about other fine books and
calendars from Westcliffe
Publishers, please contact
your local bookstore, call
us at (800) 523-3692, or
visit us on the Web at
**westcliffepublishers.com**.*

**COVER PHOTO:**
A scenic horseback
ride to Spirit Lake

**PREVIOUS PAGE:**
A ride on Beatty's
Flats in the Santa Fe
National Forest

**PLEASE NOTE:**
Risk is always a factor in backcountry and high-mountain travel, and
travel with horses presents an additional set of risks. Many of the activi-
ties described in this book can be dangerous, especially when weather
is adverse or unpredictable, and when unforeseen events or conditions
create a hazardous situation. The authors have done their best to provide
the reader with accurate information about backcountry travel with horses,
as well as to point out some of its potential hazards. It is the responsibility
of the users of this guide to learn the necessary skills for safe horseback
riding and to exercise caution in potentially hazardous areas. The authors
and publisher disclaim any liability for injury or other damage caused by
backcountry traveling, horseback riding, or performing any other activity
described in this book.

The authors and publisher of this book have made every effort to ensure
the accuracy and currency of its information. Nevertheless, books can
require revisions. Please feel free to let us know if you find information
in this book that needs to be updated, and we will be glad to correct it
for the next printing. Your comments and suggestions are always welcome.

# *Acknowledgments*

We would like to thank our parents for all the support they have provided through-out our lives. Also, thank you to Big Al in Taos Ski Valley, the guys at Philmont's Livestock Department—Ben, Chuck, Rod, and Bob—and Jeff Foster back in Iowa for everything they have done for us. A big thank you to Bill, Catherine, and Juanita for putting us and our horses up every time we drive by.

Thank you to all the Public Lands Information Center, U.S. Forest Service, Bureau of Land Management, New Mexico State Parks, and New Mexico Game and Fish employees who answered so many of our questions. Thank you to the Back Country Horsemen of New Mexico and its seven chapters. They are an all-volunteer organization that works to maintain and build trails all around New Mexico. They do a wonderful job and are always looking for new members. Visit www.bchnm.org for more information.

Also, a big thank-you goes to our horses for carrying us all over New Mexico.

**Dedicated to our parents, and our horses.**

# Contents

**State Map** ........................................... 6

**Preface** ............................................. 9

**How to Use This Guide** ......................... 10

**Preparing for Your Trip** ........................ 14

**Equipment for Day Trips** ..................... 16

**Camping and Trail Ethics** .................... 18

**Safety Considerations** ......................... 20

**The Rides**

    CHAPTER ONE: Carson National Forest .... 26

    CHAPTER TWO: Santa Fe National Forest .. 146

    CHAPTER THREE: Cibola National Forest .. 182

    CHAPTER FOUR: Lincoln National Forest .. 206

    CHAPTER FIVE: Gila National Forest ....... 234

**Appendix: Public Agency Contact Information** ...................................... 264

**Index** ............................................. 267

**About the Authors/Photographers** ........ 272

OPPOSITE: Carson National Forest

# Saddle Up, New Mexico!

## The Statewide Horse Trail and Travel Guide

### LEGEND

- Carson National Forest (Rides 1 - 41)
- Santa Fe National Forest (Rides 42 - 55)
- Cibola National Forest (Rides 56 - 63)
- Lincoln National Forest (Rides 64 - 72)
- Gila National Forest (Rides 73 - 82)

- ○ City or Town
- (41) State Highway
- (54) U.S. Highway
- (40) Interstate Highway

### Symbols used on interior maps

- Paved Road
- Dirt or Gravel Road
- Ride Route
- Other Ride Routes on the same map
- Intersecting or Alternate Trail
- ▲ Campground    ▲ Primitive Campground
- TH● Trailhead
- ○ Corral, City, Town, or Feature along the ride
- Gate
- ● Water Tank or Spring
- Lake or Pond
- River or Creek

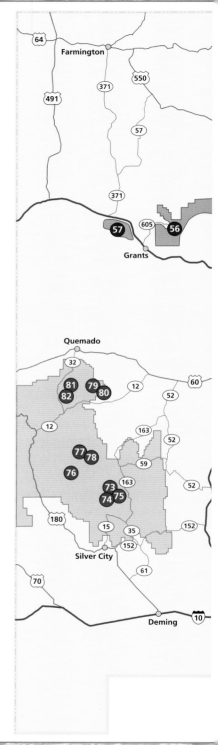

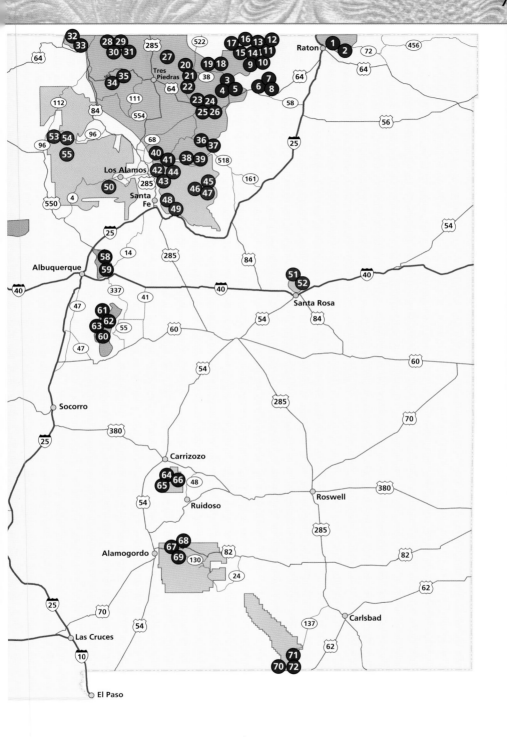

# *Preface*

"There are as many ways to do things with horses as there are horse people" is a quote we've heard from more than one old cowboy. This book proves the statement true: It by no means covers all the wonderful areas that are open to horseback riding in New Mexico, but rather offers a sampling of our favorite trails and regions. For the curious and the adventurous, there will always be more trails to discover. Our goal is to introduce you to an area, give an overview of potential rides, and provide a guide to help you decide where to go. In this book, we explain the methods that we have found most effective and safest for ourselves and our horses—recognizing, of course, that you may have found better ways for yourself. We also outline the U.S. Forest Service requirements and help you plan for both longer and shorter trips.

With its diverse, beautiful, and rugged terrain and acres of national forests and state parks, New Mexico is an ideal place for horse people, and we hope that you will find this book useful in making the most of its many miles of gorgeous trails and backcountry roads.

The Spirit Lake ride in Santa Fe National Forest

**OPPOSITE:**
Taking it easy in Cibola National Forest

# *How to Use This Guide*

The 82 trails included this guide represent some of the best riding available in New Mexico's five national forests. They are organized according to region and present a wide spectrum of terrains, elevations, and distances, allowing for trips ranging anywhere from a few hours to a few days. For each ride, we provide a map, trail description, directions, and information on facilities for both horses and riders. In addition, the following pages include important tips on preparing for a trip on horseback in New Mexico's wild areas, which are stunning, provided one is prepared for weather, the elevation, and the unexpected. This guide is as comprehensive as we could make it, but keep in mind that it does not replace the expertise of U.S. Forest Service (USFS) and Bureau of Land Management (BLM) officials, who will also be able to assist you in preparing for your trip.

## Maps

The maps in this guide will give you a basic idea of where the trails are located and what the terrain will be like. However, they are not in any way intended to be the only maps you take into the mountains. The best type for outdoor exploration are topographical maps that show terrain changes in detail. We use and recommend those put out by the U.S. Geological Survey (USGS) or the USFS. Also helpful are Forest Service and BLM maps—they provide a broader overview of an area, including the trails and roads, but do not show topographical information. You can also purchase computer programs that give topographic seamless coverage of the entire state. The website www.publiclands.org is a great place to order maps, and you can obtain them at the local ranger station as well. Outdoor gear shops will also have maps for sale.

It is very important to be prepared for various terrains, which means having knowledge of the area you plan to ride in. After you look at your map and decide which type of trail fits your and your horses' conditioning levels, call or stop by a ranger station to find out about current conditions and recent events in the area, including water availability, local weather, area closings, and fire restrictions. If you live in New Mexico, you know that finding a reliable water source isn't always easy, and that often there is only enough rain to bring lightning and a new fire threat.

## Distance and Elevation

The mileage given for each ride is the round-trip distance. We determined the length of each ride by using a GPS (Global Positioning System) device and information from maps, as well as by talking to rangers. Although GPS is fairly accurate and maps and rangers are always right on the money, some of the rides may be a little shorter or a little longer than our written mileage, but not by much.

We determined elevation using the same methods we used for determining mileage. Many of the rides in this guide begin at 8,000 feet or above. If you are coming from a lower elevation, it would be a good idea to take a couple of days to acclimate to these new elevations and get used to having less oxygen. When deciding which ride is best for you, look at not only the distance but the elevation range for the trail. If the ride starts at 7,000 feet and goes up to 12,000 feet but is only 5 miles long, it is going to be a more challenging trip. However, if the length of the ride is longer, say 13 miles, it may not be as difficult despite your traveling a greater distance. Many of the rides that take you to the summits of mountains are mostly up on the way there and mostly down on the way back. Some, though, will have many ups and downs, which can greatly increase the difficulty. Make sure to read the description of the ride if you are unsure, and refer to the difficulty ratings, which will help you to determine the strenuousness of the trail.

## Difficulty Ratings

We analyzed a variety of factors in determining the difficulty rating of a ride, including elevation, terrain, and distance. The steepest trails we considered to be the most difficult. Some of the rides that are identified as moderate may be several miles longer than a strenuous ride but have much less gain in elevation. Trail condition was also considered in ratings. If, for instance, you have to dismount and lead your horse around logs more than 10 times, the ride might start to seem difficult. Some of the trails are very rocky, in which case we mention it in the description of the ride—if your horse has sensitive hooves, rocky trails may not be for you. Any ride longer than 12 miles we have labeled either moderate or strenuous, depending on elevation gain and trail condition. The rides labeled easy are usually ones that have little or no gain in elevation or are very short—that is, under 6 miles.

## Best Season and Water Availability

New Mexico is high-desert country. Sometimes we have wet winters and a wonderful rainy season in the summer, but usually not. The summer during which we researched this book followed an unusually wet winter. Several of the rides we did in the high mountains still had 5- to 10-foot snowdrifts in July! But when we suggest the best times of the year to ride in these areas, it is based on average winter snowfall and summer temperatures, not the unusually wet conditions we encountered. No matter which months we say are the best to ride in an area, however, it is always important to call the local ranger to get current trail conditions. Also, some of the lower-elevation rides may be scorching hot in the middle of the summer, while the higher-elevation rides may be more likely to see afternoon thunder and lightning storms. Call the local ranger for more information and advice on how best to prepare for the weather conditions.

When considering water availability, remember that streams are usually either flooding or drying up in New Mexico. So if you were hoping to either cross a stream or use it as your water source, call the ranger first. Also, as we discovered, wells dry up and water pipes break and the campgrounds that we promise will have water might have had an accident, so, again, call ahead.

Trampas Lake in Santa Fe National Forest

Many of the campgrounds are closed before Memorial Day and after Labor Day. It is always a good idea to confirm with the ranger district that the area you want to stay in is open and the water is turned on.

## Shoes

Our horses were shod for every ride in this book. Usually, we do not take our horses trail riding unless they are shod. Every rider, though, has his or her own reasons to shoe or not to shoe. We like to shoe because of the variable terrain in New Mexico. A trail may be billed as a lovely grassy meadow, but often the tall grass hides sharp rocks. Or even if the ride is a nice sandy road, there may be a rocky section in the parking lot that you have to cross to get there, and our pampered, spoiled horses have sensitive hooves. However, we have marked several rides for which your horse wouldn't need shoes. In these cases, the meadow truly is soft grass and there are no rocks to cross on the way to that sandy road.

## Traveling in Wilderness Areas

Federal law states that a wilderness is "an area where the earth and its community of life are untrammeled by man, where man himself is a visitor who does not remain." On September 3, 1964, President Lyndon B. Johnson signed into law the Wilderness Act, which created the National Wilderness Preservation System. This official designation grew out of the country's first wilderness area in southwest New Mexico, designated in June of 1924 with the help of Aldo Leopold.

Wilderness areas are open only to foot travel or horseback, making them very popular with horsemen looking for areas to ride with no mountain or dirt bikes. However, wilderness areas also lack piped water, toilet facilities, and any other improvement except trails and trail signs. When traveling and camping in wilderness areas, you should use the "leave no trace" methods discussed in other areas of this book. Generally, group size is limited to 25 people, but the recommendation is 10 or less. Some wilderness areas also limit the number of stock allowed in one group and the length of stay allowed.

# *Preparing for Your Trip*

## Getting In Riding Shape

Many people who don't ride have no idea how strenuous a long day on horseback can be. If you and your horse have had a long winter of lounging around, it is a good idea to prepare physically for your trip. Nothing ruins a ride faster than having a sore horse one day into a seven-day trip. Horses need to strengthen their backs and you may need to get those riding muscles into shape again as well. If you plan to do horse packing or any other activity that is unfamiliar to your horse, make sure to practice in a familiar area before heading to the trail. This will make you more comfortable and will decrease your chances of having a wreck.

There are a few factors to consider when taking a horse into the mountains. Many of the trails in New Mexico are at a higher elevation, and if you live at a lower elevation, it may take both you and your horse a day or two to acclimate to the change. It would not be a good idea to drive in from Oklahoma and the next day expect your horse to carry you to the top of Wheeler Peak. Also, you will want to consider the condition of your horse's hooves and how recently he has been shod. Will you be able to replace a shoe if your horse throws one? Has your horse had experience crossing streams, maneuvering around different obstacles like logs or rocks, encountering wild animals or backpackers, being highlined or hobbled, or caught in bad weather?

A cowboy once told us, "There are only two things a horse is afraid of: things that move and things that don't move." For the safety of all, please remember that anything can happen in the woods, and while accidents shouldn't haunt your dreams, awareness of hazards should be in the back of your mind while you prepare for your trip and should make you cautious at all times while riding.

## Traveling With Your Horse

It is important to make sure your truck and trailer are in good shape before you travel. Check the lights and the spare tires—dirt mountain roads can be deadly to a tire. If you don't have a compressed air tank or tire repair kit, you might consider investing in one. A trailer caddy is a handy tool for changing a tire on trailers with two tires per side. It is also crucial that your truck is big enough to safely haul your trailer when filled with horses. It is dangerous to you, your horses, and other drivers if your trailer is too big for your truck. You will also want to inspect the inside of your trailer before every use. Make sure the floor is solid, and check that the mats are in place and secured. You should check all edges and ensure that nothing could cut your horse.

Your horses should be familiar and comfortable loading and unloading from the trailer. When you are loading up after dark at an unfamiliar trailhead in the middle of a thunderstorm, you will want to know that your horses are comfortable moving in and out of the trailer. Use some sort of shipping boots or polo wraps to protect your horses' legs while traveling. There is nothing worse than driving three hours to a trail only to find that your horse is cut up and you are unable to ride. We also use face masks when traveling in a stock trailer or when the windows are open, to help keep dust out of the horses' eyes. We generally keep the windows open in our trailer for the fresh air. Blankets are also a good idea when traveling in colder weather.

> **Planning ahead:**
> • Exercise both yourself and your horse.
> • Do some pre-trip training to familiarize your horse with anything that may come as a shock to him on the trail.
> • Get your horse shod and prepare a shoeing kit to bring along.

Often, it is not safe or practical to unload your horses during a long haul, but we always try to stop at least every three to four hours for about 30 minutes. This gives the horses a chance to stand and relax for a while. When the trailer is moving, the horses are constantly trying to stay balanced and they will appreciate the chance to just stand still. Stopping also provides a good opportunity to give them some fresh water if possible.

Some trailheads and campgrounds have limited parking and turnaround space. We accessed all the trails in this book with a 20-foot gooseneck trailer. If you have a bigger trailer, you should call the ranger office to be sure your rig will have room. If you will be traveling for more than one day, be sure to plan your trip so that you have a good place to overnight your horses. Check out the *Nationwide Overnight Stabling Directory* and *Equestrian Vacation Guide* for places to keep them.

Before you leave for the trail, you should call the district ranger office to check on local conditions, water availability, and fire and area closings. When crossing state lines into New Mexico, all horses must have a valid Coggins test. Contact your local veterinarian to do the testing. The process takes a couple of weeks, so do not procrastinate.

Different areas have different rules about bringing in feed. Some may require weed seed–free feed and others demand that you feed only processed hay and grain pellets. Contact the local ranger in the area where you are planning to travel to get this information. If you are going to have to change your horses' feed, introduce it slowly at home at least four days before beginning your trip.

# Equipment for Day Trips

## Clothing

Your clothing is of utmost importance on a riding trip. You should wear comfortable riding jeans. If your jeans are too baggy, your legs will be rubbed raw by mile 7. Wrangler jeans are particularly nice because there is no seam on the inside of the leg. A wide-brimmed hat is also important for sun and rain protection.

Comfortable riding boots are also a necessity. You should be able to walk quite a distance in them in the event that your horse comes up lame and you have to walk back to the trailer. If you wear lace-up boots, it is important to use tapaderos or a stirrup that will not hang up your leg should you get thrown. If you're camping, you will want a comfy pair of camp shoes.

The weather in New Mexico can be very unpredictable. It is vital that you carry rain gear at all times. Storms can sweep in over the mountains quickly, especially during the summer, and the temperature will often drop dramatically. Leggings, chaps, or chinks can also be very useful when trail riding. They can help keep your legs dry and also protect them if you must go through brush.

It is a good idea as well to carry a small repair kit with some basic items. Strips of leather and some clips to rig a broken rein may save you a 5-mile walk back to camp.

Also, always have a first-aid kit in your saddlebags.

## Types of Equipment

It is important to have a saddle that is comfortable for both you and your horse. You should break in any new gear before you use it on a long trip. Many of the trails include a number of ascents and descents, and it is often necessary to use a breast collar to keep your saddle from slipping backward. Most mules and even some horses will also need a coupler to prevent the saddle from slipping forward when going downhill. It is a good idea to stop often and readjust your gear as needed. The type of saddle pad you use is crucial in preventing injury to your horses. While there are many types of pads, our best recommendation is to use one your horse is accustomed to —don't try out new gear for the first time on a long or unfamiliar trail. We also like to ride with a rope halter underneath our headstalls so that when we stop and need to tie up the horses, the halter and lead rope are already there.

Saddle and horn bags are very useful when trail riding, giving you a place to carry your lunch, water, camera, and first-aid kit. However, just because you have lots of room does not mean that you should fill it all. Saddlebags sit far back on the horse, and if they are too heavy or lopsided, they can sore your horse.

Trail ethics state that you should not lead your horse to a stream to drink, but rather bring water to your horse, which you can do with a collapsible bucket. However, it is usually fine to do so if a sandy or rocky path leads to water or if the source is man-made. Water from the stream does not need to be purified for your horse, but you should always purify it for your use by boiling it, using iodine or purifying tablets, or using a water filter. It is good to check with a ranger to get current water conditions before heading out with the hope that the stream on the map will meet all your water needs. It is common for water sources to dry up in New Mexico.

We like to use nose bags to feed our horses grain. That way, they don't drop any on the ground, and we can better monitor how much grain each horse is eating. We also keep a set of easy boots available in the chance that we cannot easily change a shoe. However, we do not use them regularly—only in emergencies.

## Horse Equipment

Saddle
Breast collar and flank cinch
Headstall
Saddle pads and blankets
Halter and lead ropes
Shoeing equipment/easy boot
Collapsible water buckets
Feed buckets or nose bags
Saddlebags
Hay and grain
First-aid kit (horses and people)
Fly spray
Hoof pick
Hoof conditioner

## Your Equipment

Riding jeans
Riding hat
Thin, long-sleeved shirt
Rain slicker and rain pants
Chaps or chinks
Jacket or sweater
Boots
Snacks (saddlebag-sized)
Water (4 quarts per day)
Repair kit
Map and compass
Emergency gear (lighter, knife,
    cell phone, and toilet paper)

# Camping and Trail Ethics

## Camping Ethics

The U.S. Forest Service publishes a helpful booklet called "Horse Sense" that details all of the ways to be ethical while camping with horses. We recommend obtaining this booklet, but since it is designed more for back-country camping with horses, we also outline some corral and car-camping tips. Dispersed camping is one of the best ways to enjoy New Mexico's national forests with horses. You can set up camp where you see a nice place, as long as it is within 300 feet of the road. Keep in mind that these sites will likely not have the amenities of a designated campground, such as corrals, purified water, or toilets. Check with the Forest Service regarding restrictions and regulations for dispersed camping before you set out.

When we camp in an area without corrals, we set up a portable electric fence. We feel it is safer and more comfortable for the horses and more environmentally friendly if done correctly. Depending on the land and vegetation, you might want to move the fence every night in order to reduce impact on the land. If you are going to tie your horses, highline them using tree-saver straps, rather than tying them to a tree. Keep the horses far enough away from the tree so they are not tearing up the roots. The U.S. Forest Service booklet covers this and also has other ways to safely overnight your horse while keeping environmental impact to a minimum. Familiarize yourself and your horses with these techniques before heading out.

If you are car camping, all of your food and dishes need to be put away in the truck or trailer. Wild animals like to eat dog food and grain. We have learned our lesson twice: first by having to chase a bear out of camp, and then by finding holes chewed into the grain sacks. We always store our animals' food in the back of the trailer at night. If you plan on camping in the backcountry, you will need to get information on bear ropes and food safety procedures from the ranger district.

## Trail Ethics

If you go through any gates, someone will have to dismount to open them. Once all the horses are on the other side, wait until the gate is closed and the rider back on his horse before getting started again. If you begin riding before the person has a chance to close the gate and remount, the horse may be nervous and jumpy about being left by his buddies and it may be harder to mount up again. Always, always close gates that were closed when you got there.

If you come across any ruins or historical remains of homesteads, or if you find fossils, arrowheads, or pottery shards, wilderness ethics as well as the law say to leave them where you found them.

Always stay on the trail. Sometimes a shortcut up a switchback looks tempting, but if a human can cause erosion and create a new trail, imagine what a horse can do.

You are bound to meet up with other people on the trail. They may be on foot or bike. They may be day hiking or backpacking. Whatever they are doing, there are a variety of things that could scare your horse. The first thing you should do when you see them coming is to say hello. Hopefully, they say hello back, so your horse knows they are human. Horses have the right-of-way, so the hikers or bikers should stand off the trail and let you pass. It is best that they stand on the downhill side of the trail. This way, if your horse does spook, he will jump uphill instead of cartwheeling down the hillside. Remember to thank people for moving out of your way.

## Trail Etiquette and Camping Tips

- Familiarize yourself with ways to safely overnight your horse in an environmentally friendly way.
- Know the current water conditions in the area you plan to travel to.
- Always expect and plan for the worst weather; it pays to be prepared.
- Let someone know what your itinerary is and then stick to it.
- Be polite to hikers and backpackers. Wave and say hello so that your horse knows they are not monsters with humps.
- If you open a gate, close it.
- Stay on the trail. Tromping all over devastates vegetation and causes erosion.
- Be "bear aware" by keeping your camp clean and hanging smelly things 10 to 15 feet high.
- Do not wash dishes, use the toilet, or set up your horse area within 100 feet of water.
- Find an area with good grazing where the horses will not tear up the ground.
- Try to keep your horse area relatively clear of dangers like deadfall and sharp rocks and debris.
- Pack out all trash.
- Always leave it better than you found it.

# *Safety Considerations*

## Trail Safety

This may seem like a no-brainer, but always lean forward when going up steep inclines and lean backward when descending. When going under low branches, always lean forward, not back. When navigating dense areas where trees are lining the trail, watch out for your knees by either steering your horse away or pushing off the tree as you get closer. If you are too close to steer away from the tree, turn your horse's head toward the tree rather than away: This will naturally turn his body away from the tree.

Do not be too shy or too macho to get off your horse in a sticky situation. If the trail becomes really steep or the rock steps are too high, it is easier for both horse and rider if the horse is led over tricky places. If you will be leading him for an extended amount of time, attach a lead rope instead of leading by the reins. (We ride with hand-tied rope halters that can be left on under the headstall and then bring lead ropes along.) Because the Forest Service is so poorly funded and the Back Country Horsemen of New Mexico association needs more volunteers, many of the trails have not been maintained in years. Expect and be prepared for deadfall and overgrown trails. If you can clear debris off the trail, you will save the Forest Service and future riders and hikers some trouble. Often

EE Canyon in the Gila National Forest

it is just a matter of pushing things to the side, but it is even a good idea to carry a small handsaw for stubborn branches if you plan on riding in areas not regularly maintained.

If one of the horses in your party loses its calm for any reason and is bucking and having a fit, or gets loose and is running free, quickly get off your horse and attach a lead rope and wait for the other horse to calm down. Keep the people in your party together and stay calm.

After a long, hot summer ride, it is a good idea to let your horses cool down before giving them any food. Some horsemen believe that water should also be withheld until they are cool, but we think a little water is just what a hot and thirsty horse needs. However, you do not want to just unsaddle and leave them with a huge tank of water. Some quick slurps from the stream on the way back to the trailer should be good until they have cooled down. A good way to judge if a horse is cool enough is to feel its chest or the inside of its rear legs and check for a normal body temperature. Feeding a horse while it is still hot can cause digestive problems that can, in turn, lead to colic.

Be aware of hunting season and popular hunting areas. If you find yourself in a campground full of hunters, it is a good idea to go and talk with them. Find out where they are planning on hunting and when. This is for your safety as well as theirs.

## Lost Horse

What could be worse than waking up to find your horses gone? There are several things you can do to prevent this. Make sure your horses are used to being highlined or kept in an electric fence. Try tying bells to their necks at night. (Be sure to tie them high and fairly tightly under the jaw so the horse cannot catch them on anything or hurt himself.) Hobble their front legs. Use a picket line tied to their foot. Tie up the most dominant member of the herd and hope the others stick around. If you do all this and they still get away, get on your hiking boots, grab a couple of nose bags, and go looking. Chances are, they are as nervous as you are and are waiting to be found and fed.

## Lost Human

The first way to ensure you don't get lost is to always carry a map of the area and a compass or GPS device. However, since GPS devices can break down, they aren't always accurate and are also dependent on getting a good signal, so make sure to have a backup map with you. The maps in this book are just guides to give an idea of the trail. They are by no means meant to take the place of a comprehensive map that will keep you from getting lost.

In our descriptions of the rides, we often refer to trail signs. Even a trail sign, though, is not a guarantee of location. Signs can get turned around and point the wrong way, and sometimes they even disappear. When approaching a trail intersection, always check your map and compass direction.

Make sure that someone, somewhere, knows where you are and when you plan on being back. This way, if you do not show up, that person will worry and know where to look for you. Horses generally know their way back and if given their head will lead you back to the trailer. Also, streams and canyons many times lead back to civilization. However, if you are unsure of your horse's ability to find the trailer or are hesitant to follow a stream or canyon, the best thing to do is stay put. Hug a tree, as they say, and let your rescuers come to you.

## Wildlife

New Mexico is home to a variety of wildlife. The larger species include elk, mule deer, bighorn sheep, cougars, black bears, and wolves. There are also javelinas, coyote, and bobcats. Mule deer and elk are a fairly common sight and in the higher elevations you may spot sheep. Black bears, wolves, and cougars are typically very shy and are a rare sight. The smaller critters you might see in higher elevations include marmots and pikas, both of which hibernate most of the year. Cute, skittish members of the rabbit family, pikas are hard to spot but are a treat if you do see one. The marmot is a high-elevation version of a groundhog and is also known as "whistle pig" or "whistling pig". You will understand the nickname as soon as you hear one screeching as it hurries to hide in its den. If you look to the sky, you will likely spot large birds, including a variety of hawks, ravens, turkey buzzards, and, if you are very lucky, a majestic golden eagle.

Black bear

# Valle Vidal

The Valle Vidal ("Living Valley") Unit of the Carson National Forest, located just south of the Colorado border and west of Raton, is a great area for both day rides and pack trips. A hundred thousand acres in size and home to the state's largest elk herd, the unit is administered by the Questa Ranger District and is indeed a special place—perhaps the best area in all of New Mexico to go horseback riding. Located in the Sangre de Cristo Mountains, the Valle Vidal is especially good for riding because of its high-mountain meadows and lack of trails. Most of the Valle lies at about 8,000 feet in elevation and as a result can have very unpredictable weather. Afternoon thunderstorms are common in the summer. The temperature can drop below freezing during the night at any time of year, and snow is not uncommon at higher elevations all summer long.

The area that is now the Valle was once part of a huge land grant made in 1841 by Mexican governor Manuel Armijo to Carlos Beaubien, a trader, and Guadalupe Miranda of Taos. Eventually, Beaubien's son-in-law, Lucien Maxwell, was able to consolidate the rights of other heirs, selling the entire area for $1.25 million. The Maxwell Grant and Railroad Company was incorporated in 1870 and reorganized as the Maxwell Land Grant Company in 1880. In the 1920s, the 200,000 acres were purchased a group of sportsmen, who renamed it the Vermejo Park Club. Later, this property and the surrounding areas were purchased by a Texas oil magnate, who combined it into units known as Vermejo Park and W. S. Ranch. After his death in 1973, the Vermejo Park Corporation (a subsidiary of Pennzoil) purchased the 492,500-acre ranch, and nine years later, in 1982, Pennzoil donated 100,000 acres to the American people and it became the Valle Vidal Unit of the Carson National Forest. Ted Turner now owns the remainder of Vermejo Park and the W. S. Ranch.

Two routes access the Valle. From the east, turn off US 64 onto Cerrososo Road 4.5 miles northeast of Cimarron. Follow Cerrososo Road for approximately 21 miles to the boundary of the Valle. The road is a gravel road with a speed limit of 25 mph, so allow plenty of time with your trailer. It can also be very dusty, and we usually use face masks to help keep the dust out of our horses' eyes. The access to the west is from the towns of Costilla and Amalia. Turn east off NM 522 onto NM 196. The boundary is located approximately 17 miles from the junction, and some of the road is paved. It is important to remember that there are no services in the Valle, so make sure you bring all the supplies you need with you.

The Valle Vidal has two seasonal closures, one in winter and one in spring, for the protection of wildlife populations. The eastern part is closed from January 1 until March 31. This is where most elk spend the winter. They must spend high amounts of energy in order to maintain body heat, and during the winter, forage is not as nutritious or plentiful. Human disturbances stress them to the point where they are more vulnerable to disease, predation, and exposure. The western part is closed from May 1 to June 30. This is where the elk cows calve. Forcing elk to less desirable calving areas results in calves with less chance of survival. Human disturbances can also cause the cows to abandon or abort their calves. FR 1950, the main road through the unit, is open for through traffic during the seasonal closings, although not maintained during the winter, and backcountry travel is prohibited.

### Camping and Horse Facilities

There are two campgrounds in the Valle: McCrystal and Cimarron. McCrystal is located 8 miles from the eastern boundary on FR 1950. Cimarron is approximately another 10 miles on FR 1950 and then 1 mile on FR 1910, or 10 miles from the western edge of the Valle. Toilets and individual parking spaces are available at both campgrounds. Drinking water is available at Cimarron, while McCrystal has water tanks for stock. Both campgrounds have many campsites for users with stock. At McCrystal, there are hitching posts and tie racks, while Cimarron Campground has small corrals. When using these campgrounds, you are required to keep your stock in these designated areas. The stay limit is 14 days, and both campgrounds make excellent starting areas for a variety of trips. Both also have fees.

Besides camping in designated campgrounds, backcountry camping is available in all areas except within 0.5 mile of open roads, within 100 yards of natural water sources, and within 300 yards of all man-made water sources.

Approximately 2 miles past Cimarron Campground are the Clayton Corrals. You can overnight your horses here but no camping is allowed. The corrals are divided into multiple areas and could support more than one group of riders. However, no water is available at this set of corrals and the Forest Service recommends that you use the campsites' horse facilities whenever possible.

## Wheeler Peak Wilderness

The Wheeler Peak Wilderness, administered by the Questa Ranger District, includes almost 20,000 acres. The elevation ranges from 7,650 to 13,161 feet, the highest point in New Mexico. Many of the trails in the area are located near or above tree line, so being aware of the changing weather is very important.

Because of its elevation, the Wheeler Peak Wilderness is one of the only areas in the state to see an alpine mat, as opposed to the grasses that usually grow in the New Mexico high country. The mat produces small bunches of tiny, colorful flowers that cover the hillsides and decorate the trails.

The Wheeler Peak Wilderness is home to Taos Ski Valley, which started out as Twining, a small mining town that sprung up in the late 1800s. In the early 1950s, Ernie Blake spotted the valley from his plane, and in 1955, he and his wife, Rhoda, founded and created what is now a popular ski resort and recreation area.

The Wheeler Peak Wilderness can be accessed from both Taos Ski Valley and Red River. From Taos Ski Valley, take NM 150 until it dead-ends in the Taos Ski Valley parking lot. The trailhead is located on the upper level of parking. From Red River, NM 578 takes you south to the trailhead.

### Camping and Horse Facilities

Twining Campground, located at the trailhead for Bull-of-the-Woods Pasture and next to the parking area for Taos Ski Valley, is not really good for horses. A better bet would be to pack up to Bull-of-the-Woods (see ride 23, p. 93) and ride from there; otherwise, you should plan on doing day rides from the parking lot.

No camping is allowed at the trailhead on the Red River side.

## Latir Peak Wilderness

The Latir Peak Wilderness, administered by the Questa Ranger District, covers 20,506 acres and includes three peaks over 12,500 feet. The wildlife and vegetation found here is similar to that found in the Wheeler Peak Wilderness. Like much of northern New Mexico, the area was once occupied by Native Americans, then Spanish explorers, followed by miners, loggers, and finally ranchers.

The Latir Peak Wilderness is accessed by taking NM 563 northeast out of Questa, then following FR 134 to the trailhead for Cabresto Lake.

### Camping and Horse Facilities

A small campground is located at the end of FR 134A next to Cabresto Lake. You could use this campground, but you would need to pack up to it, as the road is inaccessible for trailers. Another option would be to camp at a set of shipping pens 50 yards past the junction with FR 134A.

## Hopewell Lake and Cruces Basin Wilderness

The Tres Piedras Ranger District covers about 354,000 acres in the San Juan Mountains and oversees both the Hopewell Lake area and the Cruces Basin Wilderness. The elevation in this region varies from 7,000 to 10,900 feet and supports a variety of wildlife and plants. The trees are mostly piñon and juniper in the lower elevations, with ponderosa pine and aspen dominating as you go higher. Up past 9,000 feet, look for a mixed forest of spruce, fir, and aspen.

The Hopewell Lake area is full of aspen trees and is beautiful anytime, but is spectacular in the fall when the leaves change color. The lake is about 15 miles west of the town of Tres Piedras on US 64. It is an open area with no designated trails, but is great for exploring and creating your own ride.

The Cruces Basin Wilderness covers 18,900 acres in the northwest portion of the district. It is located approximately 42 miles northwest of Tres Piedras and is accessed by FR 87. An open, rolling mountain basin cut by several perennial streams, the area features large, grassy, open meadows in the lower elevations, while the higher-elevation ridges are lined with a tree mix of spruce, fir, and aspen. Like the Hopewell Lake area, there are no designated trails here, but it is a great place for people who seek solitude and want to make their own trail.

### Camping and Horse Facilities

 Three campgrounds are available in the district. All three are maintained, but only Hopewell has drinking water. The campground at Hopewell Lake is a fee area and has two small corrals within the campground. There is also a set of shipping pens off of US 64 west of the campground entrance. It is possible to keep your horses here when the lessees are not using them. Keep in mind, though, that there is no water at the pens.

Las Lagunitas and Rio de los Pinos Campgrounds do not have fees. Rio de los Pinos Campground is east of the Cruces Basin Wilderness and used mainly by anglers, while Las Lagunitas Campground is located on the southern edge and offers a decent place to camp while riding in the wilderness. A series of small

The Escondido Creek ride

# Opportunity Trail

## Sugarite Canyon State Park

**1**

| | |
|---:|:---|
| 5 miles | **Round-Trip Distance** |
| 7,500–8,200 feet | **Elevation Range** |
| Easy | **Difficulty** |
| May through October | **Best Season** |
| Corrals at trailhead | **Horse Facilities** |
| Lake Maloya, Lake Alice Campground | **Water** |
| Yes | **Shoes Needed** |
| Raton USGS 7.5-minute quad | **Maps** |
| A beautiful lake | **Special Attractions** |

## Directions to Trailhead

From Raton, take NM 72 east. Follow NM 72 approximately 3.5 miles to its intersection with NM 526, turning left (north) on 526. You will see the visitor center. Continue past Lake Alice Campground and turn left (west) at the sign for Soda Pocket Campground. The horse corrals are 1 mile up this road. The trailhead for Opportunity Trail is directly across the road from the corrals. If you are just doing a day ride, stay on NM 526 until you come to a parking area on the west side of the dam. This is where the Opportunity and Ponderosa Ridge Trails meet, and is a good place to start the ride.

This is a pleasant, easy ride taking you along the shore of beautiful Lake Maloya and through some nice mixed-pine forest. Take the trail across the road and go left (west). The start of this route is rocky, passing through scrub oak for the first 0.5 mile, but it eventually tops out in an aspen grove and then descends into a mixed-pine forest. After the switchbacks, the path then follows

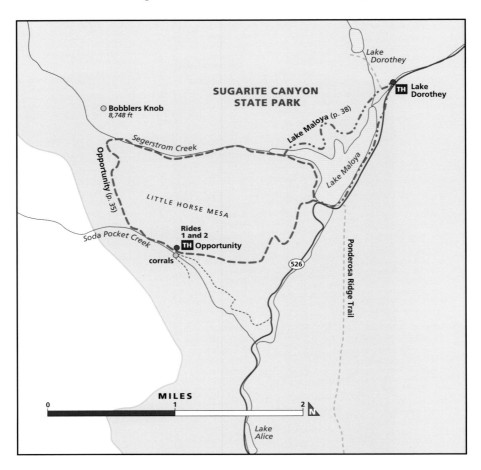

Segerstrom Valley east to Lake Maloya. At approximately 2.75 miles, the Lake Maloya Trail branches off to the left. Stay on Opportunity Trail as it parallels the lakeshore. After 3.5 miles, you come to a parking area and latrine on the west side of the dam. From here, take the Ponderosa Ridge Trail 1.5 miles back to the corrals. The trail gradually ascends through ponderosa pine forest and grassy meadows until you reach the trailhead and corrals.

# 2 Lake Maloya Trail
## Sugarite Canyon State Park

| | |
|---|---|
| **Round-Trip Distance** | 8 miles |
| **Elevation Range** | 7,500–8,200 feet |
| **Difficulty** | Easy |
| **Best Season** | May through October |
| **Horse Facilities** | Corrals at trailhead |
| **Water** | Lake Alice Campground, Lake Maloya |
| **Shoes Needed** | Yes |
| **Maps** | Raton, Yankee USGS 7.5-minute quads |
| **Special Attractions** | Gorgeous views, a beautiful lake |

# Green Mountain

## Cimarron Canyon State Park

4

| | |
|---:|:---|
| 9 miles | **Round-Trip Distance** |
| 8,300–11,160 feet | **Elevation Range** |
| Moderate | **Difficulty** |
| May through October | **Best Season** |
| Corrals at Tolby Campground | **Horse Facilities** |
| No | **Water** |
| Yes | **Shoes Needed** |
| Touch-Me-Not Mountain USGS 7.5-minute quad | **Maps** |
| Views of Eagle Nest Lake, Moreno Valley, and Touch-Me-Not Mountain | **Special Attractions** |

## Directions to Trailhead

From Eagle Nest, go east on US 64 toward Cimarron Canyon. Shortly after reaching the top of the pass and starting down into Cimarron Canyon, you will see a dirt driveway on the left. The sign indicates a reintegration center at the end of the drive. Turn onto that road and make an immediate right. On the left is a small dirt parking area. There are no signs marking the ride because it is just a road used to access the radio towers at the top of the mountain. The ride stays on the road that leads up the mountain.

This ride gradually switchbacks up Green Mountain to a set of radio towers at the top. It is nicely maintained for vehicle access, but a little rocky in places, so horses should be shod. Impressive views are the best features of this ride. As soon as you gain a little elevation, you will be able to look over your shoulder and see Eagle Nest Lake and the Wheeler Peak Wilderness. Large groups of aspen trees border the road as you go higher, which should make this ride exquisite in the fall. Once you reach the top, you can enjoy views of Capulin Volcano to the east and Touch-Me-Not Mountain to the north. A couple of broadcasting sheds and large radio towers are maintained here, so please be respectful of this property. Return to the parking area by the same route.

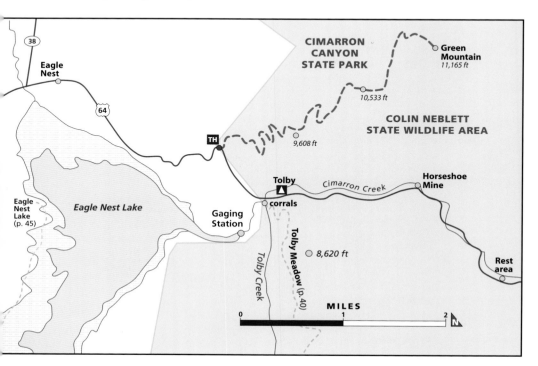

# Eagle Nest Lake

## Eagle Nest Lake State Park

**5**

| | |
|---|---|
| 8 miles | **Round-Trip Distance** |
| 8,200 feet | **Elevation Range** |
| Easy | **Difficulty** |
| May through October | **Best Season** |
| No | **Horse Facilities** |
| Eagle Nest Lake | **Water** |
| No | **Shoes Needed** |
| Eagle Nest Lake, Touch-Me-Not Mountain, Palo Flechado Pass USGS 7.5-minute quads | **Maps** |
| Easy lakeside ride, beautiful vistas | **Special Attractions** |

## Directions to Trailhead

From Eagle Nest, go 0.5 mile west on US 64 until you see the sign for the main entrance of Eagle Nest Lake State Park. Follow the dirt road down until you come to the main parking area.

The shore of Eagle Nest Lake is a relaxing ride that rewards you with stunning views of the Wheeler Peak Wilderness. From the parking area, find the break in the fence next to the bathroom. Turn right (south) and follow the lakeshore for as long as you wish. It is possible to ride to the other side of the lake, though you cannot make a complete loop because of the dam on the northeast side. Once you are riding, watch out for boggy areas close to the water. One of these bogs managed to suck the shoe off Brownie's hoof. If you are riding farther away from the lake, keep an eye out for gopher holes. You have to cross Sixmile Creek on the west side of the lake and Cieneguilla Creek on the south side. On the east side, you face the Wheeler Peak Wilderness. Here, riders can enjoy the beautiful vistas and horses the tasty grass.

## Directions to Trailhead

Follow the directions to the Elliot Barker State Wildlife Area (ride 6, p. 48).

From the corrals, simply continue down NM 204 for almost 3 miles. Take your time to enjoy and explore the meadow that stretches on either side. Soon the road passes by the site of the old Stern Ranch, where you come to a junction with a faint trail leading up to Wilson Mesa (see p. 48). Nothing remains of the old ranch now. Be sure to take a moment and notice how the burned areas are recovering.

The road crosses the creek three times, but don't feel you have to stay on it; you can go where you want in this area. If you want to continue into the Valle Vidal Unit of Carson National Forest, the trailhead begins at the locked gate at the end of NM 204. Go through the small opening in the fence and continue on the trail 0.25 mile until you pass through Rich Cabins Camp.

This is a staffed camp that Philmont uses during the summer. The cabins and outbuildings are private property and there will probably be quite a few Boy Scouts around. Continue through the camp following Middle Ponil Creek. Cross the creek and follow the old Forest Service road (see ride 14, p. 68), returning when you are ready by the same route.

## Trail Map

See p. 53.

# 8 Bonita Canyon
## Elliot Barker State Wildlife Area

| | |
|---|---|
| **Round-Trip Distance** | 4.5 miles |
| **Elevation Range** | 7,400–7,900 feet |
| **Difficulty** | Easy |
| **Best Season** | May through October |
| **Horse Facilities** | Corrals at trailhead |
| **Water** | Bonita Canyon Creek, Middle Ponil Creek |
| **Shoes Needed** | Yes |
| **Maps** | Abreu Canyon USGS 7.5-minute quad |
| **Special Attractions** | Areas burned in the 2002 Ponil Complex Fire |

# Ring Ranch

## 10

Valle Vidal Unit of Carson National Forest,
Questa Ranger District

| | |
|---|---|
| 2.5 miles | **Round-Trip Distance** |
| 8,000 feet | **Elevation Range** |
| Easy | **Difficulty** |
| May through October | **Best Season** |
| Tie racks at McCrystal Campground | **Horse Facilities** |
| McCrystal Campground | **Water** |
| No | **Shoes Needed** |
| Van Bremmer Park USGS 7.5-minute quad; USFS Valle Vidal Unit, Carson National Forest | **Maps** |
| A historic ranch | **Special Attractions** |

## Directions to Trailhead

Follow the directions to McCrystal Campground (ride 9, p. 54).

From the entrance to McCrystal Campground, follow the Ring Ranch Trail 0.5 mile until you reach the old ranch. The trail is well marked, with a slight decrease in elevation once the ranch is visible. Along the way are markers that explain the history of the area as well as the Ring family. At the ranch, more markers describe how the house was built and what life was like there over 100 years ago. Return by the same route, or take the service road back to FR 1950. Turn right onto FR 1950 and return to the campground.

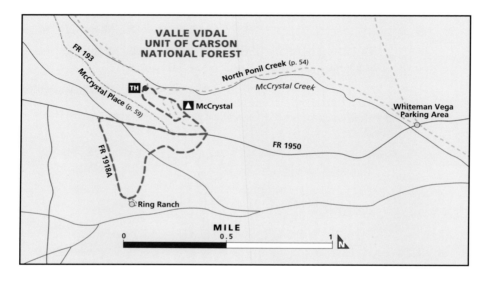

# McCrystal Place

**11**

Valle Vidal Unit of Carson National Forest,
Questa Ranger District

| | |
|---|---|
| 6.5 miles | **Round-Trip Distance** |
| 8,000–8,700 feet | **Elevation Range** |
| Easy | **Difficulty** |
| May through October | **Best Season** |
| Tie racks at McCrystal Campground | **Horse Facilities** |
| McCrystal Campground, McCrystal Creek | **Water** |
| No | **Shoes Needed** |
| Ash Mountain, Van Bremmer Park USGS 7.5-minute quads; USFS Valle Vidal Unit, Carson National Forest | **Maps** |
| The ruins of an old homestead, great views of Little Costilla Peak and Baldy Mountain | **Special Attractions** |

## Directions to Trailhead

Follow the directions to McCrystal Campground (ride 9, p. 54).

This ride takes you to the ruins of an old homestead that belonged to one of the leaders of the Colfax County War in the 1880s. John McCrystal built his house on land belonging to the Maxwell Land Grant, believing it would eventually become public domain. He soon became a leader among the anti-grant men. As the pressure on the homesteaders—or squatters, depending on which side you were on—increased, violence was often the result. Finally, John McCrystal and many of the other settlers were forced to pay the grant for the land they were using. In 1890, McCrystal paid $960 for 320 acres.

The trail is an old Forest Service road that begins behind campsite 44 and heads down to McCrystal Creek. Go through the gate by campsite 44 and then continue to the creek, turning left to follow it north. Cross the creek where the old Forest Service road does and continue along the old road. From the entrance

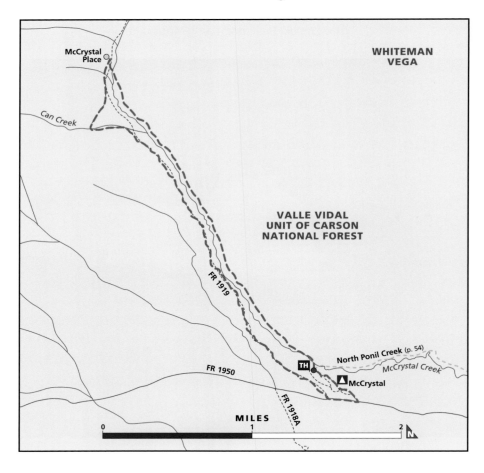

of the campground, it is about 0.7 mile across the creek to a gate. Always remember to close gates that were closed when you got there.

You will be following the creek the whole way to the ruins as it winds through a beautiful meadow with a great view of Little Costilla Peak in the distance to the west and an abundance of wildflowers all around. At about 2.3 miles, the trail comes very close to a fence. We recommend going up and around to the right and then back down into the meadow. From here, the trail peters out and you will follow the creek through the meadow to the McCrystal Place ruins in the distance. Once you are there, be sure to look south to see Baldy Mountain. Once a thriving gold mining town stood there, and now many Boy Scouts trudge to the top during their Philmont trek.

To return, follow the two-track road down the west side of the creek for approximately 3.5 miles. The road will come out on the west side of McCrystal Campground. You can go through the big swinging gates and enter directly into the campground, or follow the main road 0.25 mile east to the entrance of McCrystal Campground.

# 12 Seally Canyon

Valle Vidal Unit of Carson National Forest,
Questa Ranger District

| | |
|---|---|
| **Round-Trip Distance** | 12.5 miles |
| **Elevation Range** | 8,000–8,500 feet |
| **Difficulty** | Moderate |
| **Best Season** | May through October |
| **Horse Facilities** | Tie racks at McCrystal Campground |
| **Water** | McCrystal Campground, McCrystal Creek, a lake, five tanks along Seally Canyon |
| **Shoes Needed** | No |
| **Maps** | Abreu Canyon, Ash Mountain, Baldy Mountain, Van Bremmer Park USGS 7.5-minute quads; USFS Valle Vidal Unit, Carson National Forest |
| **Special Attractions** | Ruins of Ponil Park, Ring Ranch, a beautiful canyon |

You won't ride more than 20 minutes without a new sight on this trail, which initially takes you to the site of Ponil Park (see ride 9, p. 54) on your way to Seally Canyon. To access the trail, ride through the gates in campsites 16 or 44 and head toward McCrystal Creek, following it east on the left side until you come to the remains of an old homestead. From here, continue southeast, staying on the left side of the creek until you see a fence. Look carefully for the gate; you may have to ride the fence to find it. Once through the gate, take a right onto a Forest Service road and follow it to FR 1950. Cross the main road and continue down the service road for the next 2 miles. To view another set of homestead ruins and an old cemetery, you will want to cross North Ponil Creek at this point (see ride 9, p. 54, for directions to the cemetery and homestead site).

For Seally Canyon, continue down the old Forest Service road for about 0.25 mile until the road splits; the right fork takes you up Seally Canyon. Once in Seally, you'll almost immediately see a tank on your left, the first of five along the stream in the canyon. Seally Canyon continues approximately 4 miles west. After about 1.5 miles, you will see Seally Camp on the right, which is used by Philmont as a staffed camp for Boy Scouts in the summer.

Continue on the service road until you come to FR 1914. Take a right onto the road past the tank and almost immediately take another right off the

## Directions to Trailhead

Follow the directions to McCrystal Campground (ride 9, p. 54).

road onto a faint foot trail alongside a ditch. Follow the trail north until it hits a very old service road. This road continues through a large meadow with a lake on the right side. Along this same road, you'll see windmills and the Ring Ranch (see ride 10, p. 57). Take a right along the fence toward Ring Ranch and follow it until the second gate, which leads up the meadow toward the ranch. If you have never been to the Ring Ranch, it is worth taking some time to explore. When you are done, follow the Ring Ranch Trail back to McCrystal Campground.

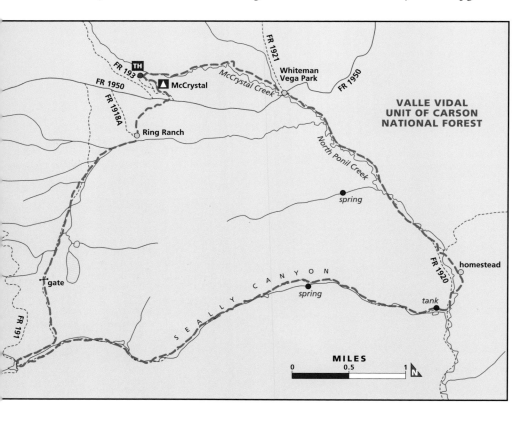

# Shuree Ponds 13

Valle Vidal Unit of Carson National Forest,
Questa Ranger District

| | |
|---|---|
| 7 miles | **Round-Trip Distance** |
| 9,200–10,000 feet | **Elevation Range** |
| Easy | **Difficulty** |
| May through October | **Best Season** |
| Cimarron Campground corrals and Clayton Corrals | **Horse Facilities** |
| Shuree Ponds, Middle Ponil Creek, Cimarron Campground | **Water** |
| Yes | **Shoes Needed** |
| Ash Mountain USGS 7.5-minute quad; USFS Valle Vidal Unit, Carson National Forest | **Maps** |
| Views of Shuree Ponds and Shuree Lodge, stunning meadows | **Special Attractions** |

## Directions to Trailhead

From the eastern boundary of the Valle Vidal Unit, follow FR 1950 west for 17 miles (passing Shuree Ponds after 15 miles) until you reach the Clayton Corrals. (About 1 mile before the corrals, you will pass FR 1910 and the turn for Cimarron Campground.)

From the western boundary of the Valle Vidal Unit, take FR 1950 east 10 miles to the Clayton Corrals. (FR 1910 and the turn for Cimarron Campground are only 1 mile farther, past the corrals. Shuree Ponds is 1 mile more.)

This is one of those rides that allows you a lot of space and opportunity to explore on your own schedule and to go where you like. We started at Clayton Corrals and followed FR 1950 to Cimarron Campground. At the east edge of the campground is a signed trail to Shuree Ponds. Follow this trail until it comes to a fence line. There is a hiker walk-through gate off to the left, but horses will have to follow the fence line to the right until it reaches an old Forest Service road. Turn left to head past Shuree Lodge to the ponds. We rode by the ponds and explored a meadow to the northeast before turning around and following FR 1950 back to Clayton Corrals.

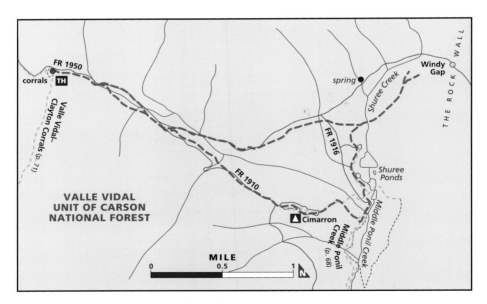

# Valle Vidal–Clayton Corrals

**15**

Valle Vidal Unit of Carson National Forest,
Questa Ranger District

| | |
|---|---|
| 9.5 miles | **Round-Trip Distance** |
| 9,400–10,000 feet | **Elevation Range** |
| Moderate | **Difficulty** |
| July through October | **Best Season** |
| Clayton Corrals | **Horse Facilities** |
| Vidal Creek | **Water** |
| No | **Shoes Needed** |
| Ash Mountain, Comanche Point USGS 7.5-minute quads; USFS Valle Vidal Unit, Carson National Forest | **Maps** |
| An old cow camp along Vidal Creek in the Valle Vidal | **Special Attractions** |

This ride through the gorgeous Valle Vidal makes clear why the area came to be known as the living valley. From the Clayton Corrals, head down the meadow on the south side of FR 1950, exploring where you want as the meadow gently slopes towards Vidal Creek. In approximately 2 miles, you come to Vidal Creek. Follow it west between two small cliffs to Clayton Camp, an old cow camp approximately 0.75 mile down the creek. (Please stay out of

## Directions to Trailhead

From the eastern boundary of the Valle Vidal Unit, follow FR 1950 west for 17 miles until reaching the Clayton Corrals and the county line for Colfax and Taos. The area west of the county line is closed to backcountry use from May 1 to June 30. About 1 mile before the corrals, you will pass FR 1910 and the turn for Cimarron Campground.

From the western boundary of the Valle Vidal Unit, stay on FR 1950 for 10 miles to the Clayton Corrals. FR 1910 and the turn for Cimarron Campground is only 1 mile past the corrals.

the old buildings.) From this area, you will see a forest administrative road heading north along Comanche Creek. Take this road approximately 2 miles until you reach a parking area along FR 1950. From this parking area, follow FR 1950 east for 3.7 miles back to the Clayton Corrals. To expand this ride, see ride 16, p. 73.

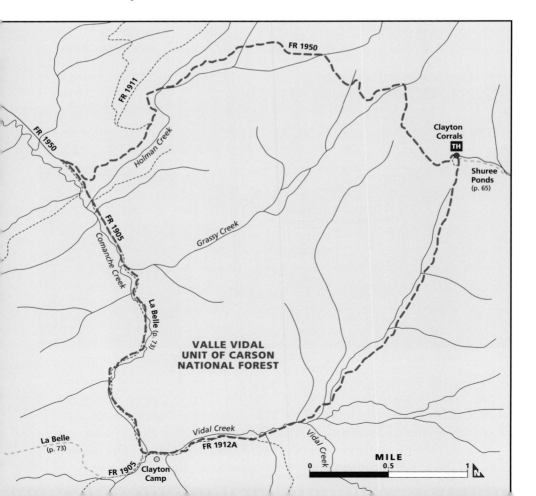

# La Belle

## 16

Valle Vidal Unit of Carson National Forest,
Questa Ranger District

| | |
|---|---|
| 6.25 miles | **Round-Trip Distance** |
| 9,200–9,650 feet | **Elevation Range** |
| Easy | **Difficulty** |
| July through October | **Best Season** |
| Corrals at Clayton Camp | **Horse Facilities** |
| Comanche Creek, stock tank at La Belle Lodge | **Water** |
| No | **Shoes Needed** |
| Comanche Point USGS 7.5-minute quad; USFS Valle Vidal Unit, Carson National Forest | **Maps** |
| Beautiful views of Valle Vidal, the site of an old gold-mining town | **Special Attractions** |

## Directions to Trailhead

Follow the directions to Clayton Corrals (ride 13, p. 65). From the east, the parking area for this ride is 3.7 miles past the Clayton Corrals on the left (south). Make the turn and continue for less than 0.25 mile to the small parking area. If you are approaching from the west, follow FR 1950 4.2 miles past its junction with FR 1900, then turn right (south). Make the turn and continue for 0.25 mile to the parking area.

From the parking area, head south on the old road that follows Comanche Creek. You will cross the creek and then pass through a gate at a little over 0.5 mile. Continue along the road, crossing the creek once more before reaching Clayton Camp and Vidal Creek at 2 miles. Head through the night trap, crossing the creek again and bearing right along Comanche Creek.

As you come around the corner of the grassy knoll after crossing the stream, you will see a very faint intersection. The more defined route heads left into a marshy area; the trail you want to stay on is fainter and heads to the right (northwest) up a small drainage to the crest of the ridge. This is an excellent place to explore if you're inclined, with an old dump complete with a rusty, wood-burning stove. Proceed along the barely visible road as it follows the crest, or simply investigate the areas that interest you. Be sure to turn around and enjoy the view of Valle Vidal to the west.

The road follows the crest toward the tree line and then bears right (north), going down and up to the other side of two small drainages. After passing through a gate, you arrive at the abandoned La Belle Lodge. Nearby is an impressive stand of quaking aspen; the wind blowing through the aspen leaves is one of our favorite sounds. In late July, this place also boasts more common

# Horseshoe Lake 18

Wheeler Peak Wilderness, Carson National Forest,
Questa Ranger District

| | |
|---|---|
| 13.35 miles | **Round-Trip Distance** |
| 9,400–12,000 feet | **Elevation Range** |
| Moderate | **Difficulty** |
| Late June through October | **Best Season** |
| No | **Horse Facilities** |
| East Fork Red River | **Water** |
| Yes | **Shoes Needed** |
| Wheeler Peak USGS 7.5-minute quad; USFS Latir Peak and Wheeler Peak Wildernesses | **Maps** |
| A high-alpine lake | **Special Attractions** |

## Directions to Trailhead

From the east side of Red River, turn south off of NM 38 onto NM 578. Follow it for 6.5 miles until the pavement turns to gravel. There are two separate parking options for this ride: A parking area is located where the pavement ends, but if your trailer is small, you could continue up the gravel road to the parking lot at the actual trailhead.

This ride is a surprisingly easy climb to a high-alpine lake, offering outstanding views and great fishing once you reach your destination. Horseshoe Lake is stocked by helicopter with native cutthroat trout, but keep in mind that a fishing license and trout stamp are required to fish here.

The first 1.5 miles of this ride follow FR 58A, also signed as Wheeler Peak Road. From the parking area at the end of the pavement, cross the bridge and bear right onto Wheeler Peak Road. Some compact trailers may be able to navigate this road; however, the parking area at the trailhead is small and space may be a problem. Stay on the road, passing some summer homes, until the East Fork trailhead. Remember, you are passing through private land, so please be respectful.

Go around the large dirt berm that marks the beginning of Horseshoe Lake Trail No. 56 and begin the gradual ascent to the lake. At about 1.8 miles, you pass the Ditch Cabin site and cross Sawmill Creek. The trail is teeming with wildflowers all summer, including cow parsnip, Nelson larkspur, Indian paintbrush, and the occasional clump of Colorado columbine. Keep an eye out for the old ditch dug in 1868, commissioned by Lucien Maxwell. It was used to carry water to the Moreno Valley for mining purposes.

After riding approximately 2.8 miles, you come to the intersection with Sawmill Park Trail No. 55, which veers off to the left. Stay on the Horseshoe Lake Trail, continuing up the canyon. Just before mile 4, you cross the East Fork of the Red River. Our horses crossed the bridge very nicely, but there is the option to go through the water on either side.

The trail continues to climb through the mixed-conifer forest. To your left, you may catch glimpses of Taos Cone and Red Dome mountains through the trees. There are two talus slopes to cross, one of which had a beautiful field of Colorado columbine blooming when we passed through. Despite the terrain, the trail across these rock fields is actually very nice.

At mile 5.5, you pass a sign letting you know you have entered the Wheeler Peak Wilderness. A half mile farther, after two stream crossings, you come to the junction of the Horseshoe Lake Trail and Lost Lake Trail No. 91. Turn left and continue 0.7 mile to Horseshoe Lake. There is one more talus slope to cross, and the trail is not as nicely maintained as the first two but should still be no problem for a decent trail horse. Closer to the lake, you may find a lot of dead-fall to navigate, and we also had to cross two large snowfields in mid-July. However, despite a couple of obstacles, the trail was wonderfully maintained and had a very gentle ascent that almost any horse would be able to manage.

Enjoy the lake, but please be careful to not damage the fragile soil around the shoreline. Let your horses graze, but keep them away from the shore. Water your horses at the stream crossing before climbing to the lake.

If you want to see New Mexico from its highest peak, take the trail on the left side of the lake up to Wheeler Peak (see ride 25, p. 98). Alternatively, you could backtrack to the junction with Lost Lake Trail No. 91 and follow it for a little over 1 mile to Lost Lake, also stocked by helicopter. This ride becomes a nice loop by continuing past Lost Lake to Middle Fork Lake Road (FR 487) and following it to Middle Fork Lake trailhead and then back to the parking area. However, Middle Fork Lake Road is used mostly by four-wheel-drive vehicles, so expect to see some motorized traffic. If you have had enough at this point, just enjoy the lake and return to the parking lot by the same trail.

## Trail Map
See page p. 84.

# 19  Sawmill Park

Wheeler Peak Wilderness, Carson National Forest, Questa Ranger District

| | |
|---|---|
| **Round-Trip Distance** | 13 miles |
| **Elevation Range** | 9,400–11,000 feet |
| **Difficulty** | Moderate |
| **Best Season** | June through October |
| **Horse Facilities** | No |
| **Water** | Sawmill Creek |
| **Shoes Needed** | Yes |
| **Maps** | Eagle Nest, Wheeler Peak USGS 7.5-minute quads; USFS Latir Peak and Wheeler Peak Wildernesses |
| **Special Attractions** | A large alpine meadow |

Sawmill Park is a relatively easy ride to a stunning high-elevation meadow. The elevation gain is about 1,600 feet, but the trail is so gentle and gradual that you will hardly notice the climb. The first 2.8 miles of this ride follow the same route as ride 18 (p. 79), beginning on FR 58A and continuing to the East Fork trailhead. After riding nearly 3 miles, you intersect Sawmill Park Trail No. 55, where the trail makes a sharp left and climbs up the east wall of the East Fork Canyon.

After passing into the Wheeler Peak Wilderness, proceed through an old gate at 3.4 miles. The trail runs parallel to Sawmill Creek, soon reaching the beginning of Sawmill Meadow, at which point it spans the creek with a nice wooden bridge that most horses should be willing to cross. If not, they should be able to cross in the water. After this crossing, the meadows begin to open up to your right as the trail continues east alongside the trees. Too much traffic in the meadow damages the marshy grasses, so please stay on the trail.

The farther along you ride, the larger the meadow becomes and the more wildflowers you will see. After 4.5 miles, the trail and meadow swing to the south. In another 2 miles, you reach Sawmill Park. The trail is easy to follow to a lone Douglas fir out in the open. From here, follow the meadow south to the saddle, stopping when you come to a fence that marks the beginning of private property. The meadow is often marshy, especially in the spring, so make sure you watch for bogs. Keep an eye out for deer and elk in the meadow and enjoy the solitude, as most hikers in the area head for Wheeler Peak and its surrounding ridges. Return to the parking lot by the same route.

## Directions to Trailhead

Follow the directions for Horseshoe Lake (ride 18, p. 79) to the parking area at the base of Wheeler Peak Road.

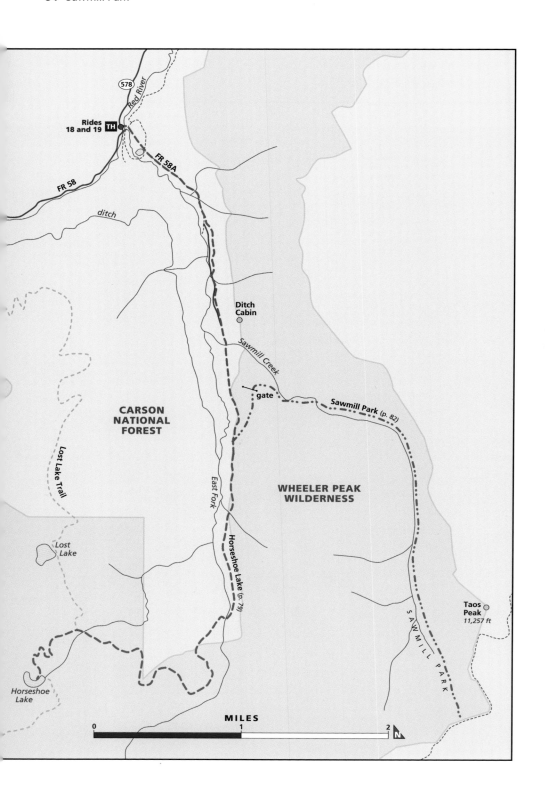

578

Red River

Rides 18 and 19 TH

FR 58A

FR 58

ditch

Ditch Cabin

Sawmill Creek

gate

Sawmill Park (p. 82)

CARSON NATIONAL FOREST

Lost Lake Trail

East Fork

WHEELER PEAK WILDERNESS

Lost Lake

Horseshoe Lake (p. 79)

Taos Peak 11,257 ft

SAWMILL PARK

Horseshoe Lake

**MILES**

0            1            2

N

# Cabresto Lake

**20**

Carson National Forest, Questa Ranger District

| | |
|---|---|
| 4 miles | **Round-Trip Distance** |
| 8,400–9,200 feet | **Elevation Range** |
| Easy | **Difficulty** |
| June through October | **Best Season** |
| Pens at FR 134A | **Horse Facilities** |
| Cabresto Lake | **Water** |
| Yes | **Shoes Needed** |
| Questa, Red River USGS 7.5-minute quads; USFS Latir Peak and Wheeler Peak Wildernesses | **Maps** |
| A wildflower-filled trip to Cabresto Lake | **Special Attractions** |

## Directions to Trailhead

From Questa, turn off of NM 522 onto NM 38 heading east toward Red River. Make a quick left onto NM 563 after 0.25 mile and continue for 2 miles, staying to the right for FR 134. FR 134 is a good all-weather gravel road but had some washboard when we drove it. Follow this road for just over 3 miles to FR 134A. FR 134A is not suitable for trailers, so take advantage of the parking at the intersection if you are planning a day ride up to the lake.

However, if you are camping, go past the junction of FR 134A 50 yards and turn left just past the cattle guard. There is also a parking area here, along with a small corral. Someone scratched "No horses allowed" on one of the boards, although the Forest Service confirms that you can use the pens as long as the lessees are not using them to round up their cattle. The Lake Fork of Cabresto Creek is also close enough to carry water to the horses in the pens.

F R 134A heads up to lovely Cabresto Lake and a nearby campground, suitable for pack trips but inaccessible by trailer. Ponderosa pine lines the road, along with cardinal flowers. It is a popular road for four-wheel-drivers going up to the lake to fish, so be on the lookout for vehicles. You might also explore the numerous shortcuts up the road that are closed to motorized traffic but suitable for horses or people on foot. Some of them are closed entirely to help preserve the soil. Please respect closed areas and go around them.

Cabresto Lake is serene and, although it is accessible by vehicles, still feels remote. Once you reach the lake, get out your fishing pole and enjoy the views. When you are ready, return by the same route.

## Trail Map

See p. 89.

# Heart Lake

## Latir Peak Wilderness, Carson National Forest, Questa Ranger District

# 21

| | |
|---|---|
| 12.5 miles | **Round-Trip Distance** |
| 8,400–11,500 feet | **Elevation Range** |
| Moderate | **Difficulty** |
| June through October | **Best Season** |
| Pens at FR 134A | **Horse Facilities** |
| Cabresto Lake, Cabresto Creek, numerous small streams crossing trail, Heart Lake | **Water** |
| Yes | **Shoes Needed** |
| Latir Peak, Questa, Red River USGS 7.5-minute quads; USFS Latir Peak and Wheeler Peak Wildernesses | **Maps** |
| Cabresto Lake, Heart Lake | **Special Attractions** |

---

**Directions to Trailhead**

Follow the directions to the parking areas for Cabresto Lake (ride 20, p. 85).

---

Head up FR 134A until it reaches Cabresto Lake and the campground (see ride 20, p. 85). Trail No. 82, the Lake Fork Trail, begins to the left of the bathroom at Cabresto Lake and heads west around the lake, eventually proceeding up the canyon following the Lake Fork of Cabresto Creek. About 2.5 miles from the Lake Fork trailhead is the junction with Bull Creek Trail No. 85. At this point, the conifer forest of cork bark fir becomes mixed with aspen, our personal favorite. Cross Bull Creek and continue up the canyon on Trail No. 82. In another mile, the trail passes several meadows as it continues to climb. Indian paintbrush, wild geranium, and bluebells decorate the trail in the summer.

At 4.5 miles from Cabresto Lake, you come to the junction with Baldy Mountain Trail No. 81. Turn left to continue to Heart Lake. The trail climbs out of the trees and soon follows the stream up to the lake. Rock cairns mark the path where the trail is scarce. Secluded and pristine, Heart Lake is a wonderful place to stop for lunch and spend some time exploring. The water is so clear that you can see rocks and fish in the shallow area near the shore. The remains of the old dam make it possible to walk around the lake. Take your time eating lunch and enjoying the beauty and solitude, but keep an eye out for building thunderstorms. Return by the same trail.

If you are doing a pack trip or want a longer day ride, consider checking out the signed trail to Baldy Mountain. You can also pick up Trail No. 85 to

Latir Mesa on the southwest shoreline of Heart Lake. Trail No. 85 is steep and difficult. Once on top of the mesa, the views are grand, but the trail fades after you emerge from the timberline and you must do a little searching for the route. It is possible, however, to do a loop and reconnect with Trail No. 82. You should have a map of the area and a compass if you plan to do this loop, and be sure to get current trail conditions and area information from the Forest Service if you plan on taking horses.

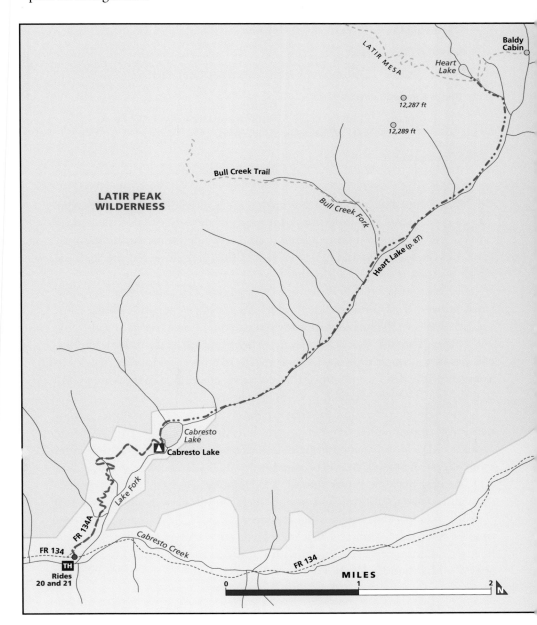

# 22 Columbine Creek
## Carson National Forest, Questa Ranger District

| | |
|---|---|
| **Round-Trip Distance** | 7.5 miles |
| **Elevation Range** | 7,900–9,900 feet |
| **Difficulty** | Moderate |
| **Best Season** | June through October |
| **Horse Facilities** | No |
| **Water** | Columbine Creek, spigots at trailhead |
| **Shoes Needed** | Yes |
| **Maps** | Questa USGS 7.5-minute quad; USFS Latir Peak and Wheeler Peak Wildernesses |
| **Special Attractions** | Fall foliage, Columbine Creek |

This is a nice ride, taking you through a series of wildflower-filled meadows as it parallels Columbine Creek for much of the way. Start in the parking area outside of the Columbine Campground and ride in, or, during less busy times of year, look for parking in the back of the campground at the trailhead, which is across from the bathrooms.

The trail crosses the creek many times along this ride, and there are three small bridges to assist hikers. The bridges are not large enough for horses, but the crossings are shallow and easy to navigate on a horse that is comfortable with water. The trail was not perfectly maintained when we rode it, and we encountered a couple of obstacles that we had to go over and under. We cleared as much of the dead wood out of the trail as we could, but chances are good that there will be new deadfall in coming seasons.

After about 1.75 miles, the trail arrives at the first of several picturesque meadows. You can either stop here or continue on toward those that follow. At about 3 miles, after passing through another meadow, the trail begins to climb more steeply, making a couple of switchbacks. It is a little rocky in places.

The next meadow you encounter is surrounded by aspen, and if you pass through it, cross the stream, and ride another 100 yards, you will find one more clearing, which is also used as a backcountry campsite. At this point, you have traveled just under 4 miles. When we visited, the clearing was filled with wildflowers and green grass. We stayed a little while to let the horses graze but were chased off by thunderclouds. Follow the same trail back to the parking lot.

## Directions to Trailhead

From Questa, travel 4 miles east on NM 38. Columbine Campground is on the right (south) side of the road. The trailhead is on the south end of the campground at the back.

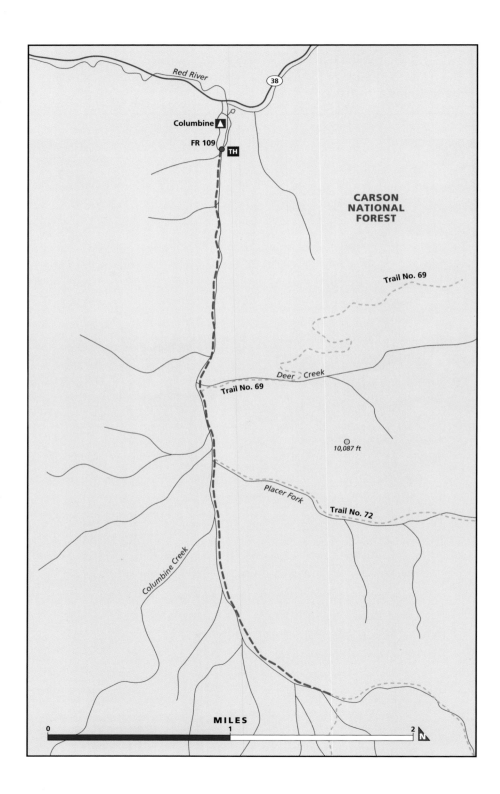

Red River

38

Columbine ▲

FR 109 ● TH

CARSON
NATIONAL
FOREST

Trail No. 69

Deer Creek

Trail No. 69

10,087 ft

Placer Fork

Trail No. 72

Columbine Creek

**MILES**

0     1     2     N

## Directions to Trailhead
Follow the directions to the Bull-of-the-Woods trailhead (ride 23, p. 93).

This loop offers dramatic views from Gold Hill, which is much more than a hill at over 12,000 feet in elevation. The trail starts in the Taos Ski Valley parking lot and follows the trail to Bull-of-the-Woods Pasture for the first 2 miles, then heads up toward Gold Hill before looping back through Long Canyon. Once you reach the pasture (see ride 23, p. 93), the trail forks in several directions, with Gold Hill on your left, the pasture straight ahead, and the Wheeler Peak trail on the right. Also to the right is a little pond where the horses can get a drink before climbing again.

Go left and begin a slow and steady climb up toward Gold Hill. You will pass through a couple of lovely meadows with great photo opportunities of Taos Ski Valley and Wheeler Peak behind you. Continue up this trail until you emerge from the timberline and can see Gold Hill before you. The ruins of an old log cabin from mining days stand on the right as you get closer to the rim. The Long Canyon Trail, which takes you back toward the Bull-of-the-Woods Trail, is due west of the old cabin and marked by cairns. Continue up the Gold Hill Trail until you top out and are looking down at Goose Lake. From here, you can ride down to Goose Lake, ride to the top of Gold Hill, or begin heading down Long Canyon. If you want to go to the summit of Gold Hill, follow the cairns. Otherwise, enjoy the views of Goose Lake, then return to the old cabin to pick up the Long Canyon Trail straight west of the site.

The first part of the Long Canyon Trail travels along the edge of a steeply sloping hillside and is very narrow, so be careful! Soon you will find a stream running alongside you on the right. As the stream becomes larger, it offers some good areas to water your horse. This stretch of the trail is lush and green—full of wildflowers and butterflies and cooled by the stream cascading down the canyon. It's approximately 4.5 miles from Gold Hill to the start of Long Canyon where the trail once again intersects the path to Bull-of-the-Woods Pasture. You can either take a right toward the parking lot or head left back up into Bull-of-the-Woods Pasture.

## Trail Map
See page p. 95.

# 25 Wheeler Peak

Wheeler Peak Wilderness, Carson National Forest, Questa Ranger District

| | |
|---|---|
| **Round-Trip Distance** | 14 miles |
| **Elevation Range** | 9,200–13,161 feet |
| **Difficulty** | Strenuous |
| **Best Season** | July through September |
| **Horse Facilities** | No |
| **Water** | Rio Hondo, Bull-of-the-Woods Pasture, Middle Fork Red River |
| **Shoes Needed** | Yes |
| **Maps** | Wheeler Peak USGS 7.5-minute quad; USFS Latir Peak and Wheeler Peak Wildernesses |
| **Special Attractions** | The highest peak in New Mexico, spectacular 360-degree views |

## Directions to Trailhead

Follow the directions to the Taos Ski Valley in ride 23 (p. 93). Park in the Bear level for access to the trailhead and to load and unload livestock.

This ride takes you to Williams Lake, a high-alpine lake filling a cirque carved out long ago by a receding glacier. Although the ride is not long and does not gain substantial elevation, the trail is a little rocky in places, causing us to rate it as moderate. This is a very popular hike, and it is unlikely that you will have the trail to yourself unless you go early or late in the season. We rode it most recently on a Sunday afternoon in July, and very rarely were we not in view of another group of people. We had also tried to hike to Williams Lake a couple of years before on Memorial Day weekend and were turned back by over 3 feet of snow.

From the Bear parking level, head past the guardhouse and turn right onto Ernie Blake Road. Follow this road for 100 yards, then bear right using the service entrance to the ski valley to cross the Rio Hondo, staying to the left around the ski lodge. Follow the foot trail underneath the ski lift and turn left onto a gravel road that is used as a return trail during ski season. Follow this road as it climbs alongside the Rio Hondo for the next 1.5 miles. You will pass by the Bavarian and Phoenix restaurants and cross under another ski lift. From here, the trail is very well marked and you should not have any problems staying on it.

After passing the Phoenix, continue for 0.25 mile on the gravel road as it parallels the river. Bear left, following the signs for Williams Lake. In approximately 0.5 mile, the road enters the Wheeler Peak Wilderness, at which point it becomes a trail. Note the stands of Engelmann spruce and the avalanche chutes as you pass; the impressive power of avalanches is made clear when you see what they have done to the trees.

The trail steadily climbs for a little over a mile as it passes a couple of huge boulder fields deposited by the same glaciers that formed Williams Lake. When you come to the top of a small rise, look down to see Williams Lake below you. A small trail follows the western edge of the lake and will take you to a waterfall. Enjoy the views and then return by the same trail. If you plan on camping at the lake, you must set up at least 300 feet from the shore. Contact the Questa Ranger District (see Appendix, p. 264) for more information.

## Trail Map
See page p. 101.

# 27 Rio Grande Gorge
Wild and Scenic Rivers Recreation Area, BLM,
Taos Field Office

| | |
|---|---|
| **Round-Trip Distance** | 3.65 miles |
| **Elevation Range** | 6,600–7,500 feet |
| **Difficulty** | Moderate |
| **Best Season** | Year-round |
| **Horse Facilities** | Trailer parking area |
| **Water** | Spigot at trailhead |
| **Shoes Needed** | Yes |
| **Maps** | Guadalupe Mountain USGS 7.5-minute quad |
| **Special Attractions** | Breathtaking views along the Rio Grande |

## Directions to Trailhead

From the center of Questa, take NM 522 north for 2.5 miles to NM 378. Make a left (west) turn onto NM 378, which is signed for the Wild and Scenic Rivers Recreation Area. Continue on this road for 11 miles until reaching an unmarked junction. Bear left to go to the visitor center and right to head to Little Arsenic trailhead 1.5 miles farther. The road to the visitor center makes a loop and will also take you to Little Arsenic trailhead. Upon reaching the trailhead, park in the area designated for horse trailers.

This ride is short in mileage but makes up for it in steepness and spectacular views. The trail starts on the west edge of the campground by the day-use parking area and immediately starts down toward the river. Watch your hat on the first switchback; a tree branch hangs low. The trail is very steep and rocky at the start and you will really appreciate your sure-footed mount. As it continues

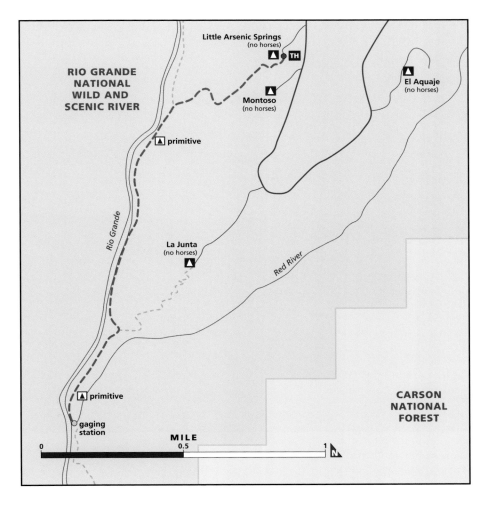

downhill, the path switchbacks down through piñon and juniper trees, some of which are over 500 years old. The Little Arsenic Trail continues for just over 0.5 mile before reaching the River Trail.

Once you reach the junction with the River Trail, turn left (south), following the Rio Grande downstream. Here, you will pass some stands of ponderosa pine, usually found only at higher elevations, as well the Little Arsenic Primitive Campground, with its small shelters. Follow the River Trail as it meanders up and down along the river.

At 0.9 mile is a junction with the La Junta Trail. Go right, continuing to head toward the confluence of the Red River and the Rio Grande. Follow the trail for an additional 0.4 mile until reaching the confluence. This is a nice area to enjoy your lunch and the views. A small footbridge, unsuitable for horses, crosses the Red River. Generally, the Red River will be uncrossable for horses unless the water level is very low. The Little Arsenic Trail is the only rim-to-river trail open to horses, so you must return by that route. If you want a longer ride, you could follow the River Trail upstream to Big Arsenic Springs and the shelters there.

## Directions to Trailhead

Follow the directions to Las Lagunitas Campground (ride 28, p. 107).

Offering a short loop through a portion of Carson National Forest, this ride does not enter the Cruces Basin Wilderness but is still extremely beautiful and well worth riding. You can use where we went as a guide, or feel free to explore the area more thoroughly.

From the lower campground, ride back to FR 87 and turn right (west). Continue on FR 87 for 1 mile until you pass through a gate next to a cattle guard, then go left (southeast) to follow Lagunitas Creek downstream. Take advantage of the small pond 0.1 mile later to water your horses. After the pond, you'll see some rock cairns and a trail marker for the Continental Divide Trail (CDT). We followed these for about 0.5 mile before leaving the trail.

Continue downstream until you find a good place to cross the small creek. On the other side of the valley are more rock cairns for the CDT. The CDT is very rocky and not well marked at this point; you may follow it or, as we did, head up to the top of the meadow where it is less rocky. We wandered through the trees at the southern edge of the meadow, eventually leaving the wooded area at mile 2.4 to overlook a deep canyon. The drop is steep but doable if your horses are comfortable with hills. If you choose to stay at the top of the canyon, follow the rim of the canyon west for 0.5 mile until you run into the boundary fence of Carson National Forest. Continue along the fence until it intersects a Forest Service road, which you can then follow back to FR 87. Turn right to continue back to the campground.

## Trail Map

See page p. 109.

# 30 Brazos Outlook

Carson National Forest, Tres Piedras Ranger District

| | |
|---|---|
| **Round-Trip Distance** | 10.8 miles |
| **Elevation Range** | 10,200–11,000 feet |
| **Difficulty** | Moderate |
| **Best Season** | June through October |
| **Horse Facilities** | No |
| **Water** | Lakes at campground, Lagunitas Creek |
| **Shoes Needed** | Yes |
| **Maps** | Toltec Mesa USGS 7.5-minute quad |
| **Special Attractions** | Views of Cruces Basin Wilderness |

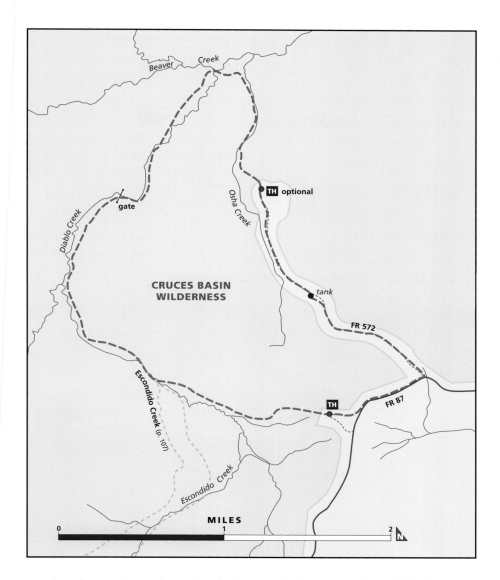

A trail worn by cattle grazing in the area heads up into Escondido Canyon. Follow the trail through some timber toward the cliffs. You come out at a large field of glacial rocks and will have a wonderful view of the cliffs on the left. Continue on the trail, following the creek, and watch for the gate on the left side of the meadow. There will most likely be cattle grazing in the area. You must cross the creek to get to the gate, but from here, you should be able to see the night-trap fence and, beyond that, the corrals. If you stay to the left of the trap, you will come to the gate that leads directly back to the corrals.

# 32 Nabor Lake

Edward Sargent State Wildlife Area

| | |
|---|---|
| **Round-Trip Distance** | 12 miles |
| **Elevation Range** | 7,900–8,500 feet |
| **Difficulty** | Moderate |
| **Best Season** | June through October |
| **Horse Facilities** | Corrals at trailhead |
| **Water** | Rio Chamita, Nabor Lake |
| **Shoes Needed** | No |
| **Maps** | Chama, Chromo Mountain USGS 7.5-minute quads |
| **Special Attractions** | Gorgeous views, a picturesque lake |

## Directions to Trailhead

From Chama, head north on NM 17. Just before leaving town, turn left (west) onto First Street. Go two blocks and turn right (north) onto Pine Street at the stop sign. Follow Pine for 0.8 mile. The road turns to gravel and then enters the Edward Sargent State Wildlife Area. Turn right into the camping and public corrals area immediately after passing through the entrance.

This ride takes you through an area that feels forgotten by time, with evidence of old homesteads emerging from the forest backdrop. From the corrals, get back on the main road that leads into the park. Turn right and follow the road until you reach the gate that blocks motorized traffic and enter the park through the small gate on the right. You will cross over Rio Chamita on a wooden bridge suitable for vehicles. It is not an ideal horse bridge because they can see through the cracks and could easily get scared, but ours did okay. The road isn't too rocky, but if you prefer, you can also ride in the meadow alongside the road or even along the river that parallels the road about 0.25 mile away.

Follow this main road for approximately 3.75 miles, keeping a lookout for a faint road on the right that leads up toward Chama Peak. It is almost easier to see the road in the distance than at its intersection with the main road. Once you turn off from the main road, Nabor Lake is about 2.75 miles farther.

Follow the faint road until you come to Rio Chamita. Here, the road is washed away, and you have to go right 100 yards or so to cross the river, but from this point, it is easy to pick the road up again. You will see the remnants of an old homestead or ranch, along with the ruins of a corral, parts of a well, and evidence of a logged area probably cut for the house that has long since disintegrated. Soon you will find that the road is lined on both sides with old, gnarled aspen trees, giving the feeling of riding down an abandoned boulevard.

No definite trail leads to the lake from this old boulevard, but if you look through the trees about 0.5 mile from the old corral, you will be able to see a meadow opening up. The lake is in this meadow. If you come to parts of an old fence, you have passed the lake. This whole area feels a bit mysterious, and if you have the time, it begs to be explored. Return to the corrals by the same route—along the road, in the meadow, by the creek, or via a combination of the three.

## Trail Map

See page p. 122.

# 33 Ridge Ride

## Edward Sargent State Wildlife Area

| | |
|---|---|
| **Round-Trip Distance** | 8 miles |
| **Elevation Range** | 8,000–9,500 feet |
| **Difficulty** | Moderate |
| **Best Season** | June through October |
| **Horse Facilities** | Corrals at trailhead |
| **Water** | Small tanks along first 2 miles |
| **Shoes Needed** | Yes |
| **Maps** | Chama USGS 7.5-minute quad |
| **Special Attractions** | Views of Chama Valley, wildlife |

## Directions to Trailhead

Follow the directions to the parking and public corrals for Nabor Lake (ride 32, p. 118).

If you are hoping to see wildlife on your ride, this little-used route through the Edward Sargent State Wildlife Area is an excellent bet. To begin, go through the opening in the fence directly north of the corrals. Once on the other side of the fence, you will see a trail winding north through the meadow, which eventually joins with a faint road. There is a tank in the meadow to the right of the road, visible by the raised mound that creates the dam. If your horses aren't thirsty yet, they'll have a couple more opportunities along the ride. In less than 1 mile, the path passes through an old fence line that runs east to west. From here and for the rest of the ride, the faint road climbs steadily but gradually. The trail is lined with a colorful assortment of wildflowers, making this an especially beautiful part of the ride.

Another tank stands on the left of the road about 1.2 miles from the corrals, and about 0.5 mile after this, you come to a virtual wall of aspen trees. They are very old and tall and tightly packed, and the forest floor is covered with ferns and cornhusk lilies. It looks like a high-desert jungle. The trail curves to the right of the aspens and then back to the left through a clearing in the trees. During the hot summer days, elk like to nap among the trees. On this ride, we saw three different groups of them. One stopped directly in front of us and watched us for a full half minute before running away. Because of the location and the lack of public use, the trail makes for great wildlife viewing.

Soon the aspen trees thin out and fir and spruce take their place as the trail gains elevation. After about 3.8 miles, the road comes to a junction, giving you the choice of making a sharp switchback to the right or continuing straight. We took the switchback right and began a steep and rocky climb to a mesa. From the switchback, it is only 0.5 mile to the top of the mesa. As you begin this climb, make sure to take in the terrific views of the Chama Valley behind and to the right of you. Watch for storm clouds as you reach the top of the mesa, as this would be a dangerous place to be caught in a thunderstorm. Return to the corrals by the same route.

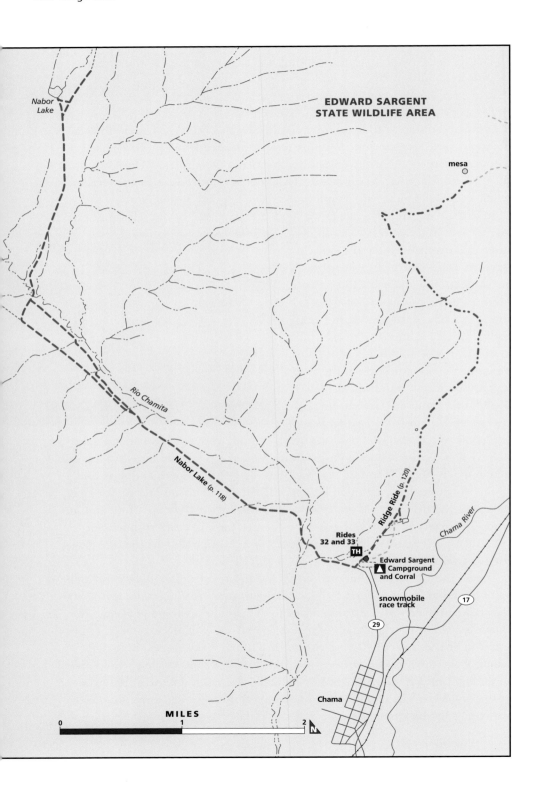

Nabor
Lake

EDWARD SARGENT
STATE WILDLIFE AREA

mesa

Rio Chamita

Nabor Lake (p. 118)

Ridge Ride (p. 120)

Chama River

Rides
32 and 33

TH

Edward Sargent
Campground
and Corral

snowmobile
race track

17

29

Chama

MILES

0     1     2     N

**Directions to Trailhead**

Follow the directions to the Hopewell Lake Campground (ride 34, p. 123).

This ride heads north along a forest road to the striking double peaks of Jawbone Mountain, and can be extended much farther if you wish. From the corrals, follow the trail toward the lake. After riding across the dam, cross the creek flowing out of the lake below the dam and then follow the wooden fence for 0.3 mile up and over the ridge until it intersects with an old, sandy road. Here, turn left (northwest) and follow the road for approximately 0.4 mile past a set of shipping pens until it comes to US 64. Cross the highway, turning left to follow US 64 for 100 yards until it reaches FR 1892 branching off to the right (north). FR 1892 is closed to vehicular traffic from May 1 to July 25 for elk calving. Go around the locked gate used to keep vehicles off the road and continue to follow FR 1892. It is also part of Trail No. 41, the Tony Marquez Trail.

At approximately mile 2.3, you will come to an intersection with another forest road. It is signed as a dead end, but looks interesting and would be worth investigating if you're inclined. If you continue straight, FR 1892 takes you along the east side of a large meadow that just begs to be explored. At 3 miles, the road passes a stand of aspen that someone has used to build a small corral. From the looks of it, we thought it would be a great place to camp with horses when the road is open to vehicles. Just past the corrals, the road is closed full-time to vehicles and open only to horses, bikes, and foot traffic. We continued on for just under 1 mile, reaching a saddle between the two peaks of Jawbone Mountain before turning around, but the old road continues much farther. Grab a topo map and continue on if you want to.

## Trail Map

See p. 125.

# 36 The Knob

Carson National Forest, Camino Real Ranger District

| | |
|---|---|
| **Round-Trip Distance** | 7 miles |
| **Elevation Range** | 8,500–10,500 feet |
| **Difficulty** | Strenuous |
| **Best Season** | June through October |
| **Horse Facilities** | Corrals at trailhead |
| **Water** | Agua Piedra Creek, Indian Lake |
| **Shoes Needed** | Yes |
| **Maps** | Jicarita Peak, Tres Ritos USGS 7.5-minute quads |
| **Special Attractions** | Gorgeous views |

## Directions to Trailhead

From Rancho de Taos, take NM 518 south for 23 miles. Turn right into Agua Piedra Campground, following the signs for the camping area. Pass the first camping area and continue on until you see the corrals. If you are just doing a day ride, park here. The trailhead is to the right of the corrals. If you are camping, the campground is just north of the corrals.

To do this ride, you should be comfortable bushwhacking. If you are not confident with directions and finding your way home, a map and compass or GPS unit would also be helpful. This trail is well worth the effort, though, as it takes you past The Knob and over to scenic Indian Lake.

The 19A trailhead is located at the corrals in Agua Piedra Campground. About 0.25 mile up the trail, you'll see a sign for Indian Lake. This is where you will return. Shortly after the sign, you come to a fence and a horse gate off to the right. The first 2 miles of this ride are challenging—steep and very rocky in places and requiring numerous stream crossings. After 1.5 miles, the trail will fork. Trail No. 22 goes right; to stay on 19A, take the left fork. After 3 miles, you top out on a little saddle. Go through the gate and watch for the trail to The Knob, which heads off to the left while 19A continues straight. The trail to The Knob and down to Indian Lake is not maintained, so there will be dead-fall on the path.

From the junction, The Knob is a little under 1 mile and you will know it when you get there. It is a small, open, rocky area with great views. The trail off The Knob to Indian Lake is very steep to begin, though it begins to level as you descend. After approximately 1 mile, you come to a large, open meadow. The trail out of the meadow is on the left toward the north end of the meadow, dropping down into another meadow where you will see Indian Lake just a short distance farther. The trail back to the corrals is on the west side of the meadow above Indian Lake and switchbacks down 1 mile to 19A. When we rode it, the trail was covered with deadfall, but we were always able to go over, under, or around. Once you reach the main trail, turn right for a short 0.25-mile ride back to the corrals.

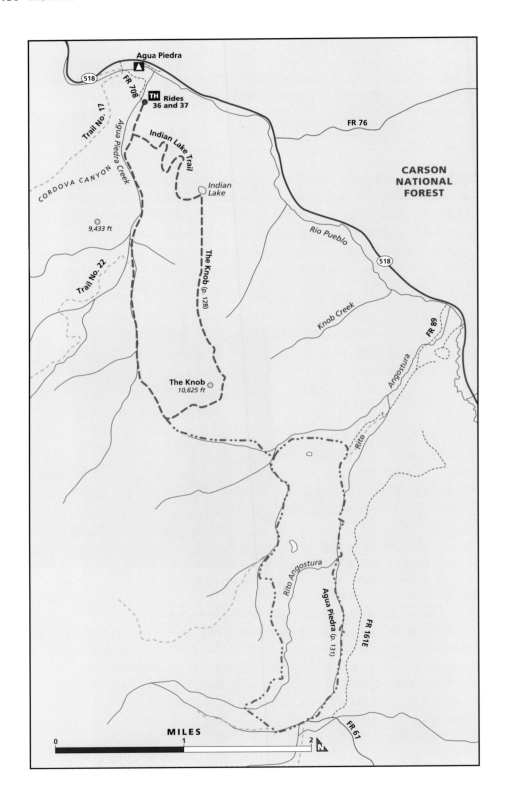

# Agua Piedra

## 37

Carson National Forest, Camino Real Ranger District

| | |
|---|---|
| 13.7 miles | **Round-Trip Distance** |
| 8,500–10,500 feet | **Elevation Range** |
| Moderate | **Difficulty** |
| June through October | **Best Season** |
| Corrals at trailhead | **Horse Facilities** |
| Multiple stream crossings | **Water** |
| Yes | **Shoes Needed** |
| Jicarita Peak, Tres Ritos, Holman USGS 7.5-minute quads | **Maps** |
| Beautiful open meadows | **Special Attractions** |

**Directions to Trailhead**

Follow the directions to the Agua Piedra Campground (ride 36, p. 128).

For the first several miles of this ride, follow the route to The Knob (see ride 36, p. 128). Instead of taking the left (northeast) turn for The Knob, however, you should continue straight on Trail No. 19A as it heads toward the south and east. The trail descends for 1 mile until it comes to a large meadow bisected by a stream. After crossing the stream, you'll see a T intersection, where you should turn right.

The trail then slowly gains elevation for another mile until it presents a short but steep climb. After the climb, you'll see a trail off to the left, which takes you to a nice meadow, if you are interested in exploring. The main trail goes straight, passing through numerous small clearings and meadows. About 1 mile after the steep climb, another unmarked trail leads to a meadow on your right. Stay straight and you'll soon come to a spot where logs were placed over a muddy spot on the trail. You may have to go around this area.

Just a short distance farther, you'll come to a stream crossing and a fork in the trail. Cross the stream and stay on the main trail as it curves around back east. As you eventually work your way toward the north, you will encounter several more forks. At the first of these, stay left, continuing until you reach FR 161. Take Trail No. 493 off to the left (north). At this point, you've ridden approximately 6.7 miles. Shortly after starting on Trail No. 493, you come to another fork. To the right is Alamitos Canyon. Again, you'll want to take the left fork, which follows a small stream. The trail gradually loses elevation for the next 2.5 miles. Be sure to watch for the little waterfall off to the left side of the trail. When you come to a big grove of aspen, take the second trail on the left, No. 3A. Follow this trail uphill for 0.75 mile, until you come back to the meadow where you originally turned right. From here, simply return back to the corrals the way you came.

## Trail Map
See page p. 130.

# 38 Middle Fork Rio Santa Barbara

Pecos Wilderness, Carson National Forest, Camino Real Ranger District

| | |
|---|---|
| **Round-Trip Distance** | 12 miles |
| **Elevation Range** | 8,900–10,300 feet |
| **Difficulty** | Moderate |
| **Best Season** | June through October |
| **Horse Facilities** | Trailer parking |
| **Water** | Spigot at trailhead, Rio Santa Barbara |
| **Shoes Needed** | Yes |
| **Maps** | Jicarita Peak USGS 7.5-minute quad; USFS Pecos Wilderness |
| **Special Attractions** | Spectacular fall colors |

## Directions to Trailhead

From Española, take NM 68 north 13.5 miles to NM 75 near Dixon. Turn right and travel on NM 75 for close to 15 miles until reaching Peñasco. Continue on NM 75 1 mile past the junction with NM 76, turning onto NM 73 while NM 75 makes a sharp left. In approximately 1.5 miles, turn left onto FR 116, which is signed for Santa Barbara Campground. Follow FR 116 for about 4 miles until you reach the campground and trailhead. From Rancho de Taos, take NM 518 south 15 miles. Turn right onto NM 75 and follow it for 5.5 miles until reaching Peñasco. Continue to the campground using the directions above.

Horses are not allowed in the campground, but trailer parking is available at the trailhead. There are no corrals here. While you can't bring your horses into the campground, you can use a portable corral or highline in the area of the old corrals. The flat area north of the trailer parking works well for this purpose. Santa Barbara is a popular staging area for pack trips into the northern part of the Pecos Wilderness.

The trail starts across the road from the trailer parking area at Santa Barbara Campground. Take Trail No. 24 as it heads south on the west side, passing through a gate and then by the water storage tank used for the campground. The trail is nice and wide and not very rocky. After 1.15 miles, you'll enter a small meadow and pass a junction with Trail No. 100, a little-used trail that you wouldn't know was there except for the sign. Continue on Trail No. 24 as it follows the Rio Santa Barbara upstream. After 1.5 miles, you pass into the Pecos Wilderness. At 0.25 mile past the wilderness sign, the trail crosses the river via a nicely constructed wooden bridge that most horses should be willing to use. You could also cross through the river if your horse is not comfortable with the bridge. After crossing, watch for the cliffs on the west side of the river.

Just past mile 2.4, you come to a junction with Trail No. 25, which bears right and continues to follow the river while Trail No. 24 turns left and heads uphill. Turn left and stay on Trail No. 24 as it gradually switchbacks up the ridge overlooking the Middle Fork of the Rio Santa Barbara. Once you are past the switchbacks, the trail will take you the rest of the way through a huge stand of aspen. The fall colors are absolutely spectacular throughout this ride. Also watch for red raspberries along the trail during the end of summer.

As the trail continues to climb, you pass through some small rockslides; fortunately, the trail through them is very accessible for horses. About 6 miles from the trailhead, the trail enters a meadow filled with cornhusk lilies. The views are wonderful here, so be sure to stop and enjoy them. If you continue through the meadow, you will come to the trail junction with Trail No. 26. We turned around at this point, although if you wanted a longer ride, you could continue up Trail No. 24 following the Middle Fork or Trail No. 26 following the East Fork of the Rio Santa Barbara.

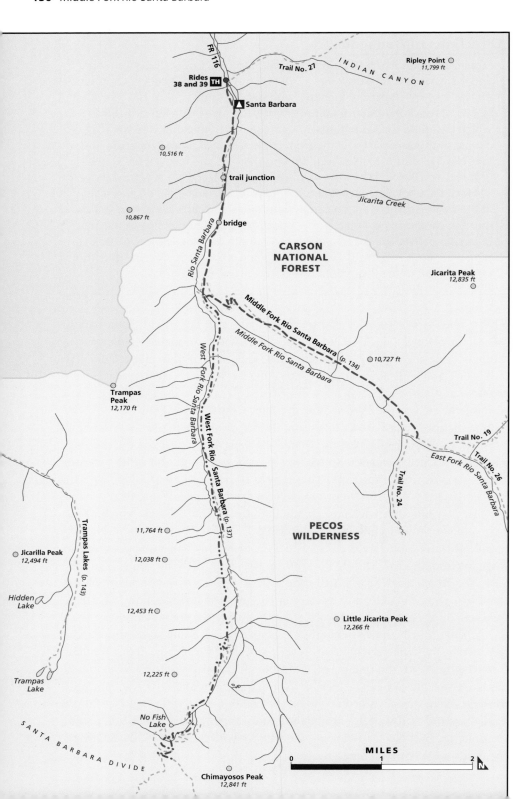

Ripley Point
11,799 ft

FR 116

Trail No. 27

INDIAN CANYON

Rides
38 and 39 TH

△ Santa Barbara

10,516 ft

trail junction

Jicarita Creek

10,867 ft

bridge

CARSON
NATIONAL
FOREST

Rio Santa Barbara

Jicarita Peak
12,835 ft

Middle Fork Rio Santa Barbara

Middle Fork Rio Santa Barbara (p. 134)

10,727 ft

West Fork Rio Santa Barbara

Trampas
Peak
12,170 ft

West Fork Rio Santa Barbara (p. 137)

Trail No. 19

Trail No. 24

East Fork Rio Santa Barbara

Trail No. 26

11,764 ft

PECOS
WILDERNESS

Jicarilla Peak
12,494 ft

Trampas Lakes (p. 143)

12,038 ft

Hidden
Lake

12,453 ft

Little Jicarita Peak
12,266 ft

Trampas
Lake

12,225 ft

No Fish
Lake

SANTA BARBARA DIVIDE

Chimayosos Peak
12,841 ft

MILES

0          1          2

N

# West Fork Rio Santa Barbara

**39**

Pecos Wilderness, Carson National Forest,
Camino Real Ranger District

| | |
|---|---|
| 20 miles | **Round-Trip Distance** |
| 8,900–12,000 feet | **Elevation Range** |
| Strenuous | **Difficulty** |
| June through October | **Best Season** |
| Trailer parking | **Horse Facilities** |
| Spigot at trailhead, Rio Santa Barbara | **Water** |
| Yes | **Shoes Needed** |
| Jicarita Peak, Pecos Falls USGS 7.5-minute quads; USFS Pecos Wilderness | **Maps** |
| Beaver dams, spectacular views, bighorn sheep | **Special Attractions** |

### Directions to Trailhead

Follow the directions and camping suggestions for Middle Fork Rio Santa Barbara (ride 38, p. 134).

This 20-mile ride, climbing in elevation to 12,000 feet as it passes through the gorgeous Pecos Wilderness, makes for a long and rewarding day. You start on Trail No. 24, which heads south on the west side of the campground (see description for ride 38, p. 134). Continue on Trail No. 24 for 2.4 miles until you reach the junction with Trail No. 25.

Here, you part ways with Trail No. 24, bearing right onto Trail No. 25, which soon takes you by two small meadows and then across the Middle Fork of the Rio Santa Barbara. After crossing the river, the trail turns back south and leaves the Middle Fork behind. Soon you hear the rushing water of the West Fork off to your right. Two miles past the junction with Trail No. 24, the path intersects Trail No. 44, which goes up over the ridge and meets up with the Trampas Lakes Trail No. 31. This junction is not marked and is not suitable for horses.

Continue to follow Trail No. 25 as it travels up the canyon, with the West Fork to your right. The trail passes through open meadows filled with wildflowers and soon rewards you with spectacular views of Chimayosos Peak

directly in front of you. About 5 miles from the trailhead, begin to watch for the large beaver dams that have backed up the West Fork. They are magnificent, but if you go over to check them out, it is probably better to leave your horse

*photo courtesy of "Big Al"*

back near the trail, as the ground is very muddy and boggy the closer you get to the dam. Mountain men based out of Taos, including Kit Carson, used to trap beaver in this very river over 175 years ago.

At 5.5 miles, the trail crosses the West Fork and begins to climb the canyon wall on the west side of the river. If you don't want to go all the way to the Santa Barbara Divide, this is a good place to turn around. Once across the river, the trail gains 2,100 feet of elevation over the next 4 miles. To continue, follow the trail as it switchbacks up the canyon. The climb is not all that hard and is made easier by the great views you are teased with as you climb. Although some maps show the trail taking you by No Fish Lake, it doesn't actually pass nearby and the lake is not visible from the trail.

The last little climb up to the divide is above tree line and takes you up a gravel slope. The trail is in good shape but not very wide, so if you see a group heading down while you are ready to go up, it is best to wait for them to pass before you begin. Once up to the divide, the views are spectacular. Be sure to bring your binoculars to look for bighorn sheep. We watched a group of nine rams not more than 50 yards away from us while we ate lunch (too bad we didn't bring the zoom lens for our camera). Many trails lead away from the divide. If interested in going farther or on a pack trip, make sure you are familiar with the trails, as there are no trail signs at the divide. When ready, return by the same route.

## Trail Map

See page p. 136.

# 40

# San Leonardo Lakes

Pecos Wilderness, Carson National Forest,
Camino Real Ranger District

| | |
|---|---|
| **Round-Trip Distance** | 8 miles |
| **Elevation Range** | 9,000–11,300 feet |
| **Difficulty** | Moderate |
| **Best Season** | June through October |
| **Horse Facilities** | No |
| **Water** | Rio de las Trampas, Rio San Leonardo |
| **Shoes Needed** | Yes |
| **Maps** | El Valle USGS 7.5-minute quad; USFS Pecos Wilderness |
| **Special Attractions** | Alpine lakes |

## Directions to Trailhead

From Española, take NM 68 north 13.5 miles to NM 75 near Dixon. Turn right (east) and travel on NM 75 for close to 14 miles until the junction with NM 76. Take a right (south) onto NM 76 and continue for 4.4 miles until reaching FR 207. Turn left onto FR 207, an all-weather gravel road. You will pass through some private land before reaching Trampas Medio Campground in 8.2 miles, though dispersed camping areas begin to appear alongside FR 207 after approximately 5.7 miles. One area even has a pit toilet. About 0.4 mile from the trailhead, you pass by a junction with FR 639 on your right. The Trampas Medio Campground is located here, although it does not allow much room for a trailer.

From Taos, take NM 518 south 15 miles. Turn right (west) onto NM 75 and follow it for 5.5 miles until reaching Peñasco. Continue for another mile until reaching the junction with NM 76 and turn left for FR 207. From here, follow the directions above to the trailhead and camping areas.

The trailhead/campground is a nice area but has limited parking and turnaround space. We got here early afternoon on a Friday in late August. There were two other cars parked at the trailhead and we had no problem getting turned around and parked. By Saturday morning, over 10 cars were parked and we would have a very hard time getting turned around.

This ride offers scenic views and pleasant riding along the Rio San Leonardo as it climbs to the pristine San Leonardo Lakes high in the Pecos Wilderness. The trail starts on the south side of the campground and is well marked by a sign. Immediately, it crosses the Rio de las Trampas and then the Rio San Leonardo. The trail is a little confusing here, but it is clearly marked by signs that will keep you headed in the right direction.

The trail heads upriver following the Rio San Leonardo, crossing it a few times. At 0.9 mile, it meets up with FR 639, where there is a small parking area for cars. The route continues on the left side of the parking area, at this point becoming an old road now closed off to vehicles. About 0.4 mile from FR 639, you pass by some barriers erected to keep vehicles off the trail. Choose your path through them carefully—some are not wide enough for a horse and both your knees.

At mile 1.7, you pass through a wooden gate and by the sign marking the edge of the wilderness. From here, the trail climbs steeply, following the river and crossing it many times in the next 2 miles. Although this ride is shorter than the ride to Trampas Lakes (see ride 41, p. 143), it is steeper and rockier and generally tougher on your horse. About 0.5 mile from the lake, the trail passes an avalanche chute and then begins the short but steep last climb to the lakes. The lower and smaller lake appears first; just continue south a short distance to the larger lake. Snow still lingered at the base of the cliffs surrounding the lake when we rode this trail in late August. Enjoy the lakes, but please keep your horses away from the fragile shore. When done enjoying the views, return by the same route. When we rode back, we chose to follow FR 639 back to FR 207 and return to our trailer by that route. Although it is longer, it is a nice ride and we enjoyed being out in the open after riding through the dense forest on the way to the lakes.

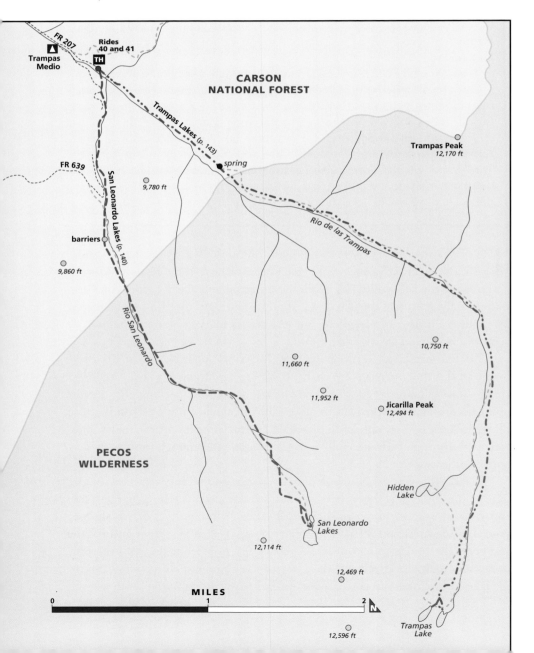

# Trampas Lakes

# 41

Pecos Wilderness, Carson National Forest,
Camino Real Ranger District

| | |
|---:|:---|
| 10.4 miles | **Round-Trip Distance** |
| 9,000–11,400 feet | **Elevation Range** |
| Moderate | **Difficulty** |
| June through October | **Best Season** |
| No | **Horse Facilities** |
| Rio de las Trampas | **Water** |
| Yes | **Shoes Needed** |
| El Valle, Truchas Peak USGS 7.5-minute quads; USFS Pecos Wilderness | **Maps** |
| Alpine lakes | **Special Attractions** |

## Directions to Trailhead

Follow the directions for San Leonardo Lakes (ride 40, p. 140) to the parking and camping areas.

This trail offers the chance to visit no fewer than three alpine lakes over the course of 10 not-so-strenuous miles. From the trailhead, start on Trail No. 31, located on the north side of the small parking area. In the first 0.2 mile, the trail passes through a wooden gate and then continues up the canyon, staying 50 or so feet above the Rio de las Trampas while it follows the river upstream. After 1.1 miles, you enter the Pecos Wilderness. Be prepared for some river crossings: The trail crosses the river just before mile 2.5 and then, in less than 0.25 mile, crosses back to the east side again.

Soon the trail begins a series of gentle switchbacks leading you past several avalanche chutes, all bearing witness to the incredible power of avalanches to shape environments. Trail No. 44 eventually branches off from No. 31, heading over the ridge where it meets up with the West Fork Trail No. 25. This junction is not marked and is not suitable for horses.

Trail No. 31 crosses the river again at 4.4 miles. Continue to climb through the forest for another 0.7 mile until reaching the junction with Trail No. 45 to Hidden Lake, which lies off to the right and a little less than a mile away. Bear left, staying on Trail No. 31, and continue another 0.1 mile to a sign directing you to the upper and lower Trampas Lakes. Both are very beautiful and worth checking out. Please keep your horses away from the shoreline to help protect the fragile area. When you are done enjoying the lakes, return to the trailhead via the same route.

## Trail Map

See page p. 142.

# Chapter Two

# Santa Fe National Forest

Pecos Baldy Lake

The Santa Fe National Forest covers 1.6 million acres and is administered by five ranger districts: Coyote, Cuba, Jemez, Pecos/Las Vegas, and Española. Also included in Santa Fe National Forest are the Dome, San Pedro Parks, Chama River Canyon, and Pecos Wildernesses. The rides we cover in this section take place in the Pecos and San Pedro Parks Wilderness Areas, two regions that offer some of the best horseback riding in New Mexico.

# Pecos Wilderness

The Pecos Wilderness is separated by the Santa Barbara Divide, with the small, northern section falling under the jurisdiction of Carson National Forest and with the southern section contained in the Santa Fe National Forest. The Española Ranger District administers the western portion, while the Pecos/Las Vegas District oversees the eastern side. This area was founded in 1892 and was known then as the Pecos River Forest Reserve. In 1915, it was combined with the Jemez Forest Reserve to form the Santa Fe National Forest. Up until the 1980s, the Las Vegas District was separate from the Pecos. Today, they form a combined ranger district, with two different ranger stations still operating.

## Camping and Horse Facilities

Campgrounds in the Pecos Wilderness range from the very popular to the hardly known. Borrego Mesa is located on the western edge of the Pecos Wilderness and is administered by the Española Ranger District. Small and little used, Borrego Mesa Campground has four tiny wooden corrals, none of which still had a gate on them when we visited. The campground itself is very pretty, nestled among an impressive stand of ponderosa pine. There is no water at the campground, so you will have to haul in all of your own. Few people use the western area of the Pecos Wilderness, almost guaranteeing that you will not see many others while in this area.

Administered by the Española Ranger District, Aspen Basin Campground consists of a few small campsites tucked into some trees in the middle of the large parking area for the Ski Santa Fe basin. The Winsor trailhead is located here and is probably the most-used trail into the Pecos Wilderness. While camping with horses is allowed, there are no good places to overnight them in the parking lot. Still, Aspen Basin offers excellent opportunities for day rides out of Santa Fe.

Pecos Canyon, located north of the village of Pecos on NM 63, offers another popular access into the Pecos Wilderness. The Pecos River flows through this canyon and a number of primitive campgrounds line the road. But just two campgrounds in the Pecos Wilderness have corrals: Jacks Creek and Iron Gate. Iron Gate is only accessed by a long and bumpy dirt road with a trailer limit of 20 feet. If you have a small enough rig and are willing to jiggle your way up the hill for 7 miles (which takes almost an hour), then the end result will be worth your effort. Not many people use the campground because of difficulty in getting there.

Jacks Creek, on the other hand, is a gorgeous and wildly popular campground that is usually packed to the gills on the weekend and cleared out completely by Sunday night. A large area, it is easily accessed by NM 63 and provides a whole separate section for campers with horses. A number of trails are nearby, and potable water and pit toilets are available. The fee to park for the day is $2 and overnight camping is $10.

## San Pedro Parks Wilderness

Administered by the Cuba and Coyote Ranger Districts, the San Pedro Parks Wilderness covers 41,132 acres, most of which lie above 10,000 feet. The area is characterized by the open meadows and green "parks" that give the region its name.

### Camping and Horse Facilities

Resumidero Campground is a big, open meadow split into a north and south section by a stream running through the middle of it. To access the north side, you would turn right onto FR 461 just before reaching the campground. The turnoff for the south area is 50 yards farther on FR 93. There are no other established campgrounds in this area, though dispersed camping is possible at the San Gregorio Reservoir trailhead.

## Rides

| | |
|---|---|
| **42** Rio Medio ......................... 149 | **49** Nambe Lake ...................... 165 |
| **43** Rio Quemado ................... 151 | **50** Rio Grande ........................ 168 |
| **44** FR 306 .............................. 153 | **51** Los Taños Equestrian Trail .... 170 |
| **45** Pecos Baldy Lake ............... 155 | **52** Salitre Tank ....................... 172 |
| **46** Beatty's Flats ..................... 158 | **53** San Gregorio Reservoir ........ 174 |
| **47** Cave Creek ........................ 160 | **54** Rio de las Vacas ................. 177 |
| **48** Spirit Lake ......................... 163 | **55** San Pedro Parks ................. 179 |

# Rio Medio  42
Pecos Wilderness, Santa Fe National Forest,
Española Ranger District

| | |
|---|---|
| 6.5 miles | **Round-Trip Distance** |
| 8,250–8,800 feet | **Elevation Range** |
| Moderate | **Difficulty** |
| June through October | **Best Season** |
| Corrals at Borrego Mesa Campground | **Horse Facilities** |
| Rio Medio | **Water** |
| Yes | **Shoes Needed** |
| Sierra Mosca, Truchas Peak USGS 7.5-minute quads; USFS Pecos Wilderness | **Maps** |
| Solitude, a river canyon | **Special Attractions** |

One of the big advantages of this ride is solitude—the western side of the Pecos Wilderness doesn't attract the crowds that neighboring regions do, allowing you to remain pretty much on your own. From the campground, take the closed dirt road that leads out of the south end. It will take you back to FR 435 and the trailhead for Trail No. 155. The trail begins behind the information board and heads downhill through a recently burned area. In the near future, deadfall will more than likely be a problem through this section of trail. The path switchbacks down to the bottom of the canyon, passing by the Pecos Wilderness boundary sign at 0.4 mile. When it reaches the bottom of the canyon, the trail turns left, heading upstream.

The trail follows the river upstream, at times coming close to the river and at other times remaining a couple hundred feet above the river on the side of the canyon wall. At mile 3.3, we chose to eat lunch and turn around at a spot directly across from some impressive cliffs. If you choose to ride farther, at about the 5-mile mark you would meet the Capulin Trail No. 158. Another mile past that is Trail No. 351 which takes you to Trailriders Wall and beyond. Be sure to check a map and get current trail conditions.

## Trail Map

See page p. 154.

## Directions to Trailhead

From Pojoaque, take NM 503 north and east for 13.4 miles. NM 503 is a narrow road as it passes through the village of Cundiyo. Immediately after the turn for Santa Cruz Lake, turn right (east) onto FR 306. Follow FR 306 for 9 miles until you reach a junction with FR 435. Turn right onto FR 435, and Borrego Mesa Campground is less than 0.25 mile down the road. The trailhead for Rio Medio Trail No. 155 is another 0.25 mile past the campground. You'll find four small corrals at the campground, all missing their gates, and will need to haul in water, as it isn't available in the vicinity.

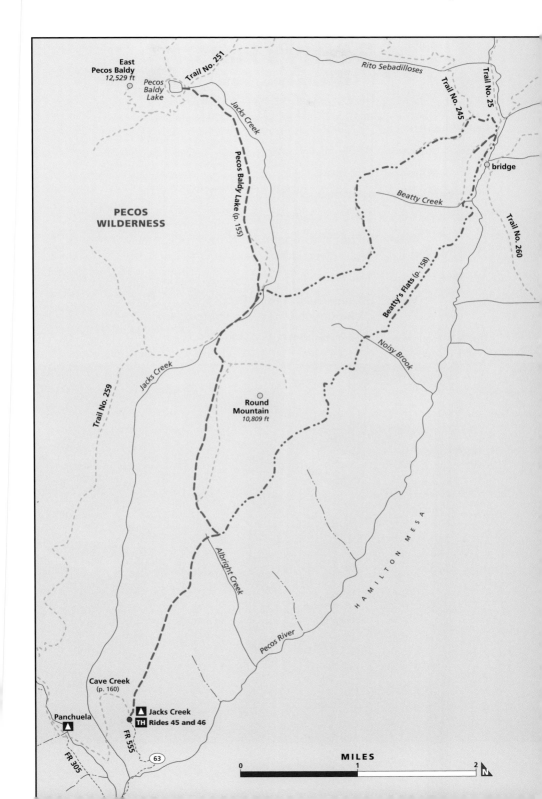

East
**Pecos Baldy**
*12,529 ft*

*Pecos
Baldy
Lake*

Trail No. 251

*Jacks Creek*

*Rito Sebadilloses*

Trail No. 245

Trail No. 25

○ **bridge**

**PECOS
WILDERNESS**

Pecos Baldy Lake (p. 155)

*Beatty Creek*

Trail No. 260

Beatty's Flats (p. 158)

*Noisy Brook*

Trail No. 259

*Jacks Creek*

○ **Round
Mountain**
*10,809 ft*

H A M I L T O N   M E S A

*Albright Creek*

*Pecos River*

**Cave Creek**
(p. 160)

▲ **Jacks Creek**
TH **Rides 45 and 46**

**Panchuela**
▲

FR 555

FR 305

63

**MILES**

0                    1                    2

N

# 46 Beatty's Flats

Pecos Wilderness, Santa Fe National Forest,
Pecos/Española Ranger Districts

| | |
|---|---|
| **Round-Trip Distance** | 15 miles |
| **Elevation Range** | 8,800–10,700 feet |
| **Difficulty** | Strenuous |
| **Best Season** | June through October |
| **Horse Facilities** | Corrals at campground |
| **Water** | Spigot at campground, Noisy Brook, Beatty Creek, Pecos River, Jacks Creek |
| **Shoes Needed** | Yes |
| **Maps** | Cowles, Truchas Peak, Pecos Falls, Elk Mountain USGS 7.5-minute quads |
| **Special Attractions** | Alpine meadows, Pecos River |

## Directions to Trailhead

Follow the directions to Jacks Creek Campground (ride 45, p. 155).

This route takes you around the base of Round Mountain and through a broad expanse of meadow, making for a long and interesting day of riding. From Jacks Creek Campground, take Trail No. 25, Beatty's Trail, out of the campground. It is marked for horses. Almost immediately, you pass the unmarked junction for Trail No. 249, which leads off to the right toward Iron Gate Campground. Stay on Trail No. 25 as it climbs steeply above the campground. After approximately 2 miles, the trail levels out and intersects with Trail No. 257, Jacks Creek Trail, bearing off to the left. This is the trail you will return on if you follow our route. Continue straight on Trail No. 25, riding along the east flank of Round Mountain. A number of small seeps keep sections of the trail fairly muddy throughout this ride.

Some older maps show Trail Nos. 26 and 27 cutting across the north side of Round Mountain, but those routes are no longer marked or maintained, so don't plan on using them as shortcuts. Approximately 4.25 miles from the trailhead, you cross Noisy Brook and 1.75 miles beyond that Beatty Creek, where the trail divides. Take the path to the right, which leads down to the Pecos River. The other trail heads directly to the Beatty's Cabin Administrative Site.

After following the river for 0.5 mile, you will see Trail No. 260 and a wooden bridge crossing the Pecos River. Shortly after the bridge, three trails (Nos. 260, 245, and 25) converge. Turn left onto Trail No. 245. Right away, another trail heads left toward the Beatty's Cabin Administrative Site. We took this trail as short side trip and thought it was well worth the extra time. Once you return to Trail No. 245, continue away from the Pecos River. In approximately 0.4 mile, you come to an intersection with Trail No. 259, the Dockweiler Trail. Watch carefully, as the intersection can be easy to miss. You will want to bear left at the intersection.

Follow Trail No. 259 for just over 3 miles until you reach the intersection with Trail No. 257, the Jacks Creek Trail. Turn left onto Jacks Creek Trail and follow it for 0.4 mile, when you will cross Jacks Creek and reach another trail junction. Stay on Trail No. 257 as it continues around the western flank of Round Mountain. About 1.9 miles from Jacks Creek, you arrive at the intersection of Trail Nos. 257 and 25. At this point, turn right and head the 2 miles back to the campground.

## Trail Map

See page p. 157.

# 47 Cave Creek

Pecos Wilderness, Santa Fe National Forest,
Pecos/Las Vegas Ranger District

| | |
|---|---|
| **Round-Trip Distance** | 7 miles |
| **Elevation Range** | 8,350–8,800 feet |
| **Difficulty** | Easy |
| **Best Season** | June through October |
| **Horse Facilities** | Corrals at campground |
| **Water** | Spigot at campground, Panchuela Creek, Cave Creek |
| **Shoes Needed** | Yes |
| **Maps** | Cowles USGS 7.5-minute quad |
| **Special Attractions** | A series of caves to explore |

## Directions to Trailhead

Follow the directions to Jacks Creek Campground (ride 45, p. 155).

This pleasant ride takes you along Cave Creek and rewards you at the end with some interesting caverns. From Jacks Creek Campground, ride below sites 7 and 8 through the meadow, heading for the road that leads into the campground. A trail cuts through the grass to the road and then continues on the other side. Follow this trail across the road and down until it meets NM 63, the main road through the canyon. Follow NM 63 south for just under 0.25 mile until you see a trail on the right (west) leading up the hill. This trail parallels the road for a short distance and then veers to the west toward Panchuela Creek. A large wooden bridge spans the creek, and since there is no other way across, your horse will have to use it, like it or not.

A short distance after this, you come to another crossing, this time through the water, and will follow the trail on the left that leads into the parking area for the Panchuela Campground. Follow the road out of the campground on the main road and look for the trail leading off to the right. When we rode, a sign indicated the route designated for horses.

As soon as you get onto the trail at around mile 1.25, you will see trail signs for Cave Creek for both riders and hikers. Take the trail signed for horses and

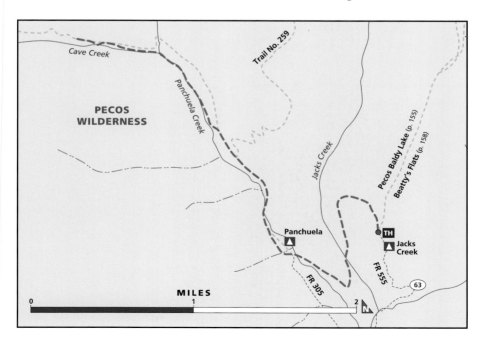

follow it as it travels above Panchuela Creek. About 0.25 mile after this intersection is another unmarked junction, with one trail leading up the mountain and the other down to the creek. Follow the trail down to the creek. Once you approach the creek, go right (southeast) along the bank until you see the easiest crossing. From this crossing, the trail leads you up a small hill and joins with the hiker trail. In another 0.75 mile, you pass by the junction with the Dockweiler Trail No. 259 branching off to the right, but stay to the left along the creek. The trail in mid-August is so filled with wildflowers that it looked like a blanket of purple and yellow, made mostly of fleabane and coneflower with an occasional monkshood.

Around mile 2.8, the trail crosses Panchuela Creek and continues west along Cave Creek. Right at mile 3.5, a small side trail leads down to the cave. Watch for a couple of false trails heading toward the creek: The side trail you want is short and you will be able to see the lip of the cave and the darkness within almost as soon as you start down it. The cave is on the opposite side of the creek. The water from the creek flows into the cave and then out again, rejoining the main body of water downstream. Farther up the trail are two even larger caves. Be cautious if you plan on entering any of them, as cowboy boots can be especially slippery on wet rocks. This is also a nice place for a break, with thick green foliage providing a canopy for shade. Return to the campground by the same route.

# Spirit Lake

**48**

Pecos Wilderness, Santa Fe National Forest,
Española Ranger District

| | |
|---:|:---|
| 11 miles | **Round-Trip Distance** |
| 10,250–11,050 feet | **Elevation Range** |
| Strenuous | **Difficulty** |
| June through October | **Best Season** |
| No | **Horse Facilities** |
| Rio Nambe, Spirit Lake | **Water** |
| Yes | **Shoes Needed** |
| Aspen Basin, Cowles USGS 7.5-minute quads | **Maps** |
| Spirit Lake, views of Santa Fe Baldy | **Special Attractions** |

## Directions to Trailhead

From Santa Fe, turn right (east) onto NM 475, signed as Artist Road and locally known as Hyde Park or Ski Basin Road. Follow this road 15 miles until it dead-ends in the Ski Santa Fe parking lot. The Winsor trailhead is located on the uppermost level, next to the bathrooms.

This popular trail takes you to an alpine lake, offering some magnificent views along the way. From the parking lot of the Ski Santa Fe basin, follow Winsor Trail No. 254 to the right. As soon as you pass the information board, cross a small bridge and begin the climb. The first 0.5 mile is probably the steepest part of the whole trail. Soon the trail comes to a fence that marks the wilderness boundary and levels out. Pass through the gate and continue straight along Trail No. 254. This part of the ride takes you through a mixture of fir and aspen and is one of the most popular hikes during the fall foliage season. The trail is rocky and the horses will have to pick their way carefully through some areas. There's some tight spots through the trees, so watch your knees!

After about 1 mile, you will pass the junction for Trail No. 403, which leads north down to the Rio Nambe. This trail is very steep and rocky and not recommended for stock. Continue along Trail No. 254. Approximately 1 mile after the junction, the path intersects with Trail No. 400, which leads up to Nambe Lake; again, stay on Trail No. 254. Right after this junction, the trail crosses the Rio Nambe and soon Santa Fe Baldy comes into view to the north. Two trails—Nos. 101 and 160—both lead to the Rio Nambe. Bypass these junctions and continue to follow the Winsor Trail all the way to Spirit Lake.

At around mile 3.75, the trail passes through a small meadow—the soft dirt here will be a welcome relief to your horses' hooves. This is also a nice place to stop for a small break and let the horses nibble some high-alpine grasses. Here, you will see the junction for Santa Fe Baldy and the Skyline Trail that leads to the left (north). Stay on 254 through the meadow where it eventually joins with the Skyline Trail No. 251 for the next mile before the Skyline Trail branches off again to the right around mile 4.25.

This last section of the trail is much like the first, with many rocks and some high steps, but our horses did fine. At mile 5.4, you come to your destination. Spirit Lake is one of many alpine lakes in the region, and because this area is so popular and close to urban areas, you will most likely see other people enjoying the scenery. Look closely into the shallow water for tadpoles. If you stay long enough and eat some lunch, you will definitely attract camp robbers, which will hop from limb to limb and make daring passes at your food. Return to the parking lot by the same route.

## Trail Map
See page p. 166.

# Nambe Lake

**49**

Pecos Wilderness, Santa Fe National Forest,
Española Ranger District

| | |
|---:|:---|
| 6 miles | **Round-Trip Distance** |
| 10,250–11,800 feet | **Elevation Range** |
| Moderate | **Difficulty** |
| June through October | **Best Season** |
| No | **Horse Facilities** |
| Rio Nambe, Nambe Lake | **Water** |
| Yes | **Shoes Needed** |
| Aspen Basin USGS 7.5-minute quad; USFS Pecos Wilderness | **Maps** |
| Nambe Lake | **Special Attractions** |

## Directions to Trailhead

Follow the directions to the Winsor trailhead (ride 48, p. 163).

The first 2 miles of this ride follow the Winsor Trail No. 254 north out of the Ski Santa Fe parking lot. At the intersection with Trail No. 400, turn right (south) toward Nambe Lake.

This part of the trail is a steep and rocky climb, following the Rio Nambe. A short distance up the trail, you should notice a trail on the left side of the river. When you can, cross the river and follow this trail. It continues to climb upward along the east side of the Rio Nambe. After leading you past a couple of small meadows, the trail crosses the river again and, from here, climbs steeply alongside some impressive cliffs. About 1 mile from the start of the Nambe Lake Trail, you reach Nambe Lake, which is situated in the basin below Lake Peak and Deception Peak. Because this is the closest alpine lake to the Santa Fe area, you are likely to see other people along the trail and at the lake. After enjoying the scenery, follow the same route back to the parking lot.

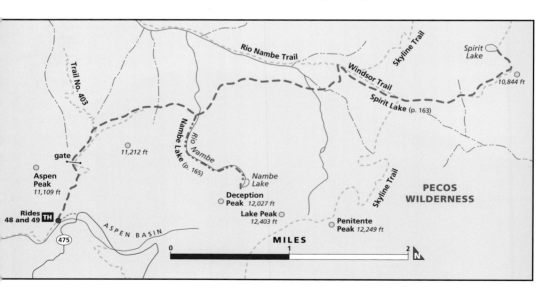

## Directions to Trailhead

Exit Interstate 40 at Santa Rosa, exit 275. Turn west onto Will Rogers Drive, then turn right (north) on North Second Street and follow the signs to Santa Rosa Lake State Park. The corrals are located in the Los Taños Primitive Camping Area.

This ride starts out of the primitive camping area and follows an easy 4-mile loop along an old service road. If you go left at the first fork, you will ride past the lake first. If you want to save the lake views for the end, then go right and enjoy the ruins of the old Reilly Ranch first. Either way, you will love this mellow ride, full of wildflowers and the wide New Mexico sky.

The loop is great if you just want a quick ride with some nice views and a guaranteed mileage. However, once you are in the primitive camping area, you can basically head your horse east and ride wherever you want within the park boundaries. It would even be possible to ride all the way around Santa Rosa Lake if the Pecos River were especially low. But it does get rocky on the west side of the lake and you would have to ride back on the pavement through all of the park's established campsites and visitor buildings.

We like this area as a place to become acclimated to new elevations, as there are no serious inclines or declines. Also, it makes the perfect stopover if you are on your way to northern New Mexico from Texas or Oklahoma, or just on a weekend trip.

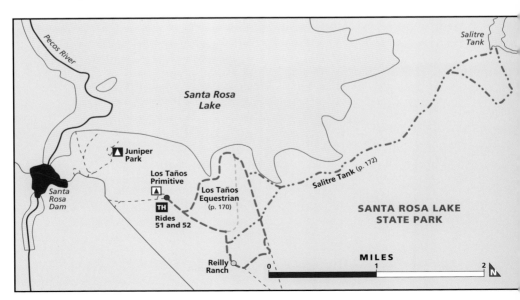

# 52 Salitre Tank
## Santa Rosa Lake State Park

| | |
|---|---|
| **Round-Trip Distance** | 10 miles |
| **Elevation Range** | 4,750–4,850 feet |
| **Difficulty** | Easy |
| **Best Season** | Year-round |
| **Horse Facilities** | Corrals at trailhead |
| **Water** | At corrals, Santa Rosa Lake, Salitre Tank |
| **Shoes Needed** | No |
| **Maps** | Catfish Falls, Sacaton Draw USGS 7.5-minute quads |
| **Special Attractions** | Santa Rosa Lake, Salitre Tank, Reilly Ranch ruins |

## Directions to Trailhead

Follow the directions to Los Taños Primitive Camping Area (ride 51, p. 170).

Starting from the primitive camping area, follow the nature trail along the old service road. The beginning of this ride follows the same path as the Los Taños Equestrian Trail and allows for many opportunities to stray from the path. In other words, it is not necessary to follow the same route that we took in order to end up at Salitre Tank. To take our route, follow the old service road along the lake and then, once it forks, go left. From here, feel free to wander: We visited an old windmill and then cut through the brush back to the trail. Stay on the trail while it veers south away from the lake; off to the left, you will see Salitre Tank. Continue along the road until you are south of the tank; at this point, feel free to leave the road and ride to the tank. The area is very lush and makes for a nice grazing break. From here, simply ride back up to the road and back the way you came. We stayed straight on the old road (heading toward power lines) and came back past the ruins of the Reilly Ranch.

## Trail Map

See page p.171.

# 53 San Gregorio Reservoir

San Pedro Parks Wilderness, Santa Fe
National Forest, Cuba Ranger District

| | |
|---|---|
| **Round-Trip Distance** | 9.5 miles |
| **Elevation Range** | 9,200–9,950 feet |
| **Difficulty** | Moderate |
| **Best Season** | June through October |
| **Horse Facilities** | No |
| **Water** | San Gregorio Reservoir, Clear Creek |
| **Shoes Needed** | Yes |
| **Maps** | Nacimiento Peak USGS 7.5-minute quad; USFS San Pedro Parks Wilderness |
| **Special Attractions** | San Gregorio Reservoir, alpine meadows |

It is a good idea to take a map and compass or GPS unit when you do this ride. The trails are not always well marked, and a number of crisscrossing cow and game trails make navigation confusing. We rode without any destination, simply exploring until we felt like turning around. If you wanted a longer ride, however, you could take this trail all the way to San Pedro Parks, approximately 9 miles from the trailhead.

The Vacas Trail No. 51 begins directly across FR 70 from the toilets. The trail climbs gradually through a mixed-conifer forest for 1 mile until reaching San Gregorio Reservoir. You will have to cross or go around two mud bridges (small logs laid over a perpetually muddy spot). The reservoir is a popular place for fishing on weekends, but once you leave it behind, you are less likely to see anyone.

The trail continues, crossing two more older mud bridges before reaching Vallecito Damian, a small meadow (the name means "Damian's little valley"), at mile 1.9. Here, a signed trail junction directs you to take a left to stay on the main trail or make a right for the Damian Trail, a new addition to the park, which would take you to the junction of the Palomas and Perchas Trails.

Continue on the Vacas Trail as it follows Clear Creek and continues north, passing through some small meadows along with heavily forested areas. Just before 3 miles, you will come to another trail junction marked by a post but no sign. We continued straight for 60 feet, then bore left at another unsigned trail junction. The trail crosses Clear Creek and follows it upstream through a meadow. Pay careful attention through this section: The trail sometimes becomes faint as it travels through the small meadows, and numerous crisscrossing cow trails make the path even more confusing. The trail tends to follow Clear Creek, so if you lose your bearings, stay close to the creek and keep your eye out for the trail as you leave the meadow. We decided to turn around after enjoying lunch in a pleasant clearing, which we shared with some grazing cows. When ready, return to the trailhead by the same route.

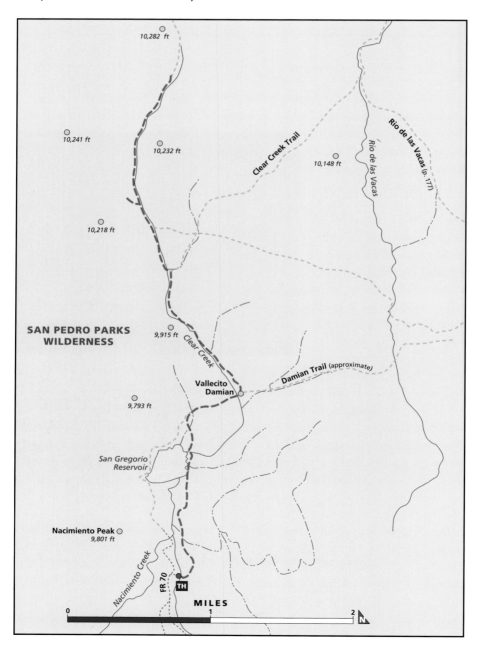

to find it again on the far sides of the clearings if you continue in that general direction. Around mile 1.45, you come to a trail junction. Trail No. 452 continues straight, while an unnamed trail turns right. Approximately 1.5 miles farther, Trail No. 452 ends at an unmarked junction with Trail No. 451, which comes down from the north. From here, you continue to travel west, though now on Trail No. 451.

Trail No. 451 heads in a west-northwesterly direction until mile 4.2, where it meets up with Trail No. 31 at an unmarked junction at the western edge of a small meadow. Turn left (south) onto Trail No. 31, which is part of the Continental Divide Trail (CDT). At this point, the trail is well marked with CDT signs. Follow the markers through the meadows at the eastern edge of

San Pedro Parks. At mile 5.9, the path intersects with the Peñas Negras Trail No. 32. If you were to turn right, it would take you to the Rio de las Vacas. Turn left onto the Peñas Negras Trail and continue for 0.1 mile until reaching the junction with the Rio Puerco Trail No. 385. Continue straight on this trail while the Peñas Negras Trail turns right (south). The route takes you through a dense forest of spruce and fir where we had to go over and around a lot of deadfall. Watching the trees for the old scars where the trail markers used to hang will help keep you on the trail.

Continue on this trail for about 2 miles until you reach a large meadow called the Vega Redonda. Here, follow the old wooden posts across the meadow and then along the dry wash. Some cow trails crisscross the meadow, making it tricky to find the Vega Redonda Trail No. 43. You will want to continue to follow the wash as it heads downhill past two beaver dams. We were not able to find the trail right away but followed the small stream on the left bank after the last beaver dam. We then saw the trail on the right side of the bank and crossed the stream to pick it up.

The trail continues downhill through more dense forest, with more deadfall. At one point, the path branches into a new and an old trail. We were able to follow the newer, better maintained trail, which switchbacks a little. If you do happen to get stuck on the old trail, it comes out at the same place as the new. Around mile 10, we crossed a meadow, following some rock cairns, crossed the stream, and then shortly joined back up with Trail No. 452 0.3 mile from the gate and wilderness boundary.

# Chapter Three

# Cibola National Forest

Mount Taylor

The Cibola National Forest is divided into four ranger districts—Mt. Taylor, Magdalena, Mountainair, and Sandia—which oversee the more than 135,000 acres contained within the Sandia Mountain, Manzano Mountain, Apache Kid, and Withington Wilderness Areas. Cibola is known for its varied terrain, ranging from rugged mountains to broad grasslands, and its numerous recreational opportunities.

## Mt. Taylor Ranger District

Mount Taylor is the highest peak in the Cibola National Forest, at 11,301 feet. An extinct volcano, it is one of many dramatic mountains in the Mt. Taylor Ranger District, which encompasses over 500,000 acres. The only access into the area is on NM 547 through Grants, where the ranger station is located.

**Camping and Horse Facilities**

No camping facilities are available in or around the Mt. Taylor District, but you can find several primitive camping sites along FR 193 on the way to the Mount Taylor trailhead.

# Sandia Mountain Wilderness

The Sandia Mountain Wilderness was created in 1978 and now includes 37,232 acres bordering the eastern edge of Albuquerque. Towering over the city, the Sandia Mountains receive heavy use during the summer and fall. The wilderness is split into north and south areas by the Sandia Peak Tramway corridor and can be accessed either on NM 14 through Cedar Crest or via the Canyon Estates trailhead just off of I-40.

**Camping and Horse Facilities**

Generally, the Sandias are used more for day trips than for overnight camping. None of the parking areas allow overnight camping. However, a newly completed horse parking area located near the Cienega Spring picnic area makes unloading easier, with a large graveled area that allows plenty of room to park and turn around a horse trailer.

# Manzano Mountain Wilderness

The Manzano Mountain Wilderness is administered by the Mountainair Ranger District and encompasses 36,970 acres. Established in 1978, the region gets its name from the old apple trees that 16th-century explorers found growing in a small village on the eastern edge of the mountains. Apples are not native to North America, and it is believed that Spanish missionaries introduced them to this region many years earlier. The village and the mountains both became known as Manzano, derived from the Spanish word for "apple."

**Camping and Horse Facilities**

Four areas have horse facilities in the Manzano Mountain Wilderness: the upper loop of Red Canyon Campground, the Pine Shadow trailhead, the Albuquerque trailhead, and the Bosque trailhead. In the upper loop of Red Canyon Campground are 10 small corrals and a stream running nearby for stock water. There is a $7 fee per night for camping, and the campground provides vault toilets, picnic tables, and campfire rings. From Red Canyon Campground, you can access the Spruce Spring Trail, Red Canyon Trail, and Ox Canyon Trail, as well as the Crest Trail.

Corrals are also located at Pine Shadow trailhead, which is 7.5 miles south of Red Canyon Campground on FR 422. There are four corrals along with a water tank for stock. When we visited, two of the gates on the corrals were missing, so you would need to be able to tie something over the entrance to keep your horses in. From the trailhead, you can access the Pine Shadow Trail up to Manzano Peak and the Crest Trail.

The Albuquerque trailhead features six corrals and a vault toilet. It is located 7.5 miles west of Tajique on FR 55. A small stream nearby provides a potential water source, but be sure to check with the Forest Service that the stream is running before counting on it. From the Albuquerque trailhead, you can access the northern end of the Crest Trail.

The Bosque trailhead is located 2 miles past the Albuquerque trailhead on FR 55. The road is not maintained past Fourth of July Campground, so be sure to check current conditions before driving there. The trailhead offers eight corrals, along with toilets, tables, and fire grates. Unfortunately, there is no water or stream nearby, so you would need to bring plenty of water for yourself and your horses. From the Bosque trailhead, you can access the Bosque Trail along with the Crest Trail, Cerro Blanco, and Trail Canyon. There are no fees for using Pine Shadow, Albuquerque, or Bosque trailheads. You are able to spend the night at each, but there are no established camping areas and few decent places for tents. We were quite comfortable sleeping in our trailer, however.

## Other Areas

### Bluewater Lake State Park

Bluewater Lake State Park is located about 100 miles west of Albuquerque just off of I-40. There are no corrals at the state park, but a large, primitive camping area is perfect for setting up an electric fence. Many people who visit the park opt to camp in the primitive area because of its proximity to the lake. While it is possible to set up right next to the lake, riders may find it easier to camp farther out along the open stretches of beach. Drinking water is available in the developed camping areas.

## Rides

| | | | |
|---|---|---|---|
| **56** Mount Taylor | 185 | **60** Albuquerque Trail | 196 |
| **57** Bluewater Lake | 188 | **61** Bosque–Cerro Blanco | 199 |
| **58** Cañoncito-Cienega | 190 | **62** Red Canyon | 201 |
| **59** South Crest Trail | 193 | **63** Ox Canyon | 204 |

# Mount Taylor

## Cibola National Forest, Mt. Taylor Ranger District

# 56

| | |
|---:|:---|
| 6 miles | **Round-Trip Distance** |
| 9,300–11,301 feet | **Elevation Range** |
| Moderate | **Difficulty** |
| June through October | **Best Season** |
| No | **Horse Facilities** |
| No | **Water** |
| Yes | **Shoes Needed** |
| Lobo Springs, Mount Taylor USGS 7.5-minute quads | **Maps** |
| Mount Taylor, scenic vistas | **Special Attractions** |

## Directions to Trailhead

From I-40, take exit 85 into Grants. Stay on Santa Fe Avenue until meeting NM 547, also known as First Street. Turn north, staying on NM 547, which will turn into Lobo Canyon Road in the middle of town next to a shopping center. Continue on NM 547 (Lobo Canyon Road) for approximately 13 miles until the pavement ends. Turn right (east) onto FR 193, an all-weather gravel road. Follow FR 193 for 5 miles to the trailhead for Gooseberry Springs Trail No. 77, marked by a small sign. There is a parking area at the trailhead. If you have a big trailer or the lot is crowded, you may need to continue on FR 193 for 0.1 mile to the junction of FR 193 and FR 501 and park there. When we rode to Mount Taylor, we camped at the junction the night before. Although there is no water, it still makes a nice place to camp. You can find several other good camping spots along FR 193, as well as a fenced-in stock tank about 2 miles before the trailhead on the right.

Mount Taylor is an extinct volcano that formed the area surrounding it. Its deposits are evident along I-40 as well as along the smaller roads around Grants. To the south of Grants is also a large lava bed, now protected as El Malpais National Monument. This amazing area is worth seeing. Because

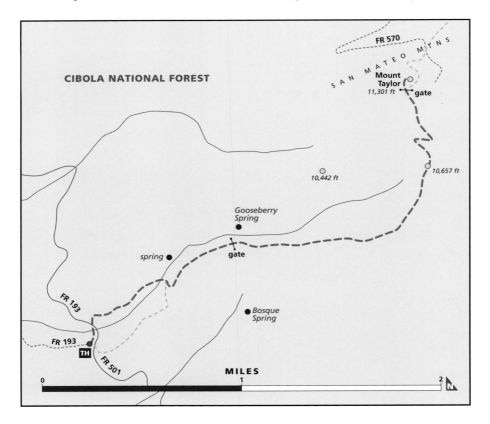

the texture of a lava bed is not good for a horse's hooves. There are only a couple of areas that are open to horseback riding. Contact the local ranger for more information.

Trail No. 77 begins across the road from a small parking area. There was not enough room for our trailer, so we drove on to the junction of FR 193 and FR 501. The junction was large enough to park and close enough to the trailhead to ride from the trailer. The first mile of the trail climbs at a moderate grade. At 0.6 mile, it drops down into a small meadow, crosses a stream, and heads to the right. After crossing the old road that used to serve as the first part of Trail No. 77, it passes through a gate at mile 1.1. The trail climbs up and out of the trees into another, larger, meadow. While you are riding up this meadow, make sure to look over your shoulder at the vista opening up behind you.

At mile 1.8, you come to a ridge at the top of the meadow. Follow the ridge to the left (north) toward the peak. Once you cross over the ridge, the trail goes up and over a small saddle and you will be able to see it switchbacking up a steep slope. The trail is a little rocky in places, but the grade remains moderate throughout the switchbacks. After 2.9 miles, the trail arrives at another gate. Once you pass through the gate, you will be able to see the peak on your right. Because Mount Taylor is the highest peak in the area at 11,301 feet, the views are amazing. Make sure to start early on this ride to avoid the late afternoon thunderstorms. When we rode it, a large, dark cloud hovered menacingly above us the whole time. Return to the trailhead by the same route.

# 57 Bluewater Lake

## Bluewater Lake State Park

| | |
|---|---|
| **Round-Trip Distance** | 6 miles |
| **Elevation Range** | 7,380–7,550 feet |
| **Difficulty** | Easy |
| **Best Season** | Year-round |
| **Horse Facilities** | No |
| **Water** | At main campground, Bluewater Lake |
| **Shoes Needed** | Yes |
| **Maps** | Pine Canyon, Prewitt USGS 7.5-minute quads |
| **Special Attractions** | Bluewater Lake |

## Directions to Trailhead

From I-40, take exit 63 at Prewitt and follow NM 412 south. Continue on NM 412 for approximately 7 miles until the road dead-ends at Bluewater Lake State Park. Take the first or second right down into the primitive camping area by the lake.

From the entrance to the state park, we took the second right and drove down to the lake and camped in the primitive area, which costs $8 per night. Horses are not allowed in the main camping area, but you are free to set up in the primitive area and ride from there. You will need either a portable corral or an electric fence, as there is no place to set up a highline. We were there on a Friday, and by the afternoon the entire beach was covered with tents and RVs. We found we had more privacy camping away from the lake at the base of the surrounding hills. From the lake, an old service road is visible heading through hills along the right (north) side of the water. We began by following this road up into the hills for the first couple of miles, paralleling the lakeshore. There are several opportunities to ride down onto the beach, but because of cliffs in the area, you may have to backtrack if you do venture closer to the water.

The road then goes away from the lake for the next mile before dropping down to the waterline. Follow the lakeshore for as long as you like. Do be careful, though, because when we went to water our horses, the mud around the lake was very deep. We followed the lakeshore for about 1 mile before returning to our trailer by the same route.

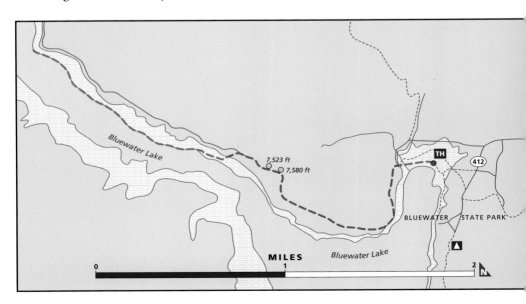

# 58 Cañoncito-Cienega

Sandia Mountain Wilderness,
Cibola National Forest, Sandia Ranger District

| | |
|---|---|
| **Round-Trip Distance** | 11 miles |
| **Elevation Range** | 7,100–9,500 feet |
| **Difficulty** | Strenuous |
| **Best Season** | Late April through October |
| **Horse Facilities** | Large parking area for trailers |
| **Water** | Stream crossing 0.6 mile from trailhead, small stream along trail |
| **Shoes Needed** | Yes |
| **Maps** | Sandia Crest, Sandia Park USGS 7.5-minute quads; USFS Sandia Wilderness |
| **Special Attractions** | Spectacular views from the Crest Trail |

## Directions to Trailhead

From Albuquerque, take I-40 east to exit 175. Follow NM 14 north for almost 6 miles until you reach the intersection with NM 536. Turn left (west) onto NM 536 and continue for 1.8 miles until reaching the turn for the Cienega Springs picnic area. Go left and then follow the signs for the Cienega trailer parking area. There is a $3 day-use fee for parking here.

This ride takes you along the scenic Crest Trail, offering gorgeous views of the Sandia Wilderness and Albuquerque beyond. From the Cienega trailer parking area, take the Cienega Horse Bypass Trail. The trail switchbacks down into Cienega Canyon while also providing glimpses of the many homes that dot the hillsides outside of national forest land. The trail passes a paved turnaround and then crosses a stream at approximately 0.6 mile, eventually climbing a small hill and meandering through the valley bottom.

A little after 1.15 miles, the trail bears off to the right; follow it down until it comes to a small stream, then turn right to continue along the stream up the canyon. The trail crosses the stream many times and continues for almost a mile before heading up what looks like a rocky wash and running into Faulty Trail No. 195. Turn left (south) and quickly drop back down to the stream. Faulty Trail crosses the stream and heads southwest.

You'll see a trail that continues straight (west) on the left side of the stream; it eventually meets up with the bypass trail. Instead of leaving the stream and climbing the short distance to meet the Faulty Trail where it is signed, you could go this way, staying alongside the stream. Many people, though, are more comfortable seeing the sign so that they are sure of where they are.

Continue on the Faulty Trail to the junction with Cañoncito Trail No. 150. Here, turn right and enter the Sandia Mountain Wilderness. It is 3 miles to the Crest Trail according to the trail signs, although we measured it at closer to 2 miles. The trail becomes rocky and steep right away, and in many areas is more like a dry wash than a trail. It climbs more than 1,600 feet before it reaches the Crest Trail. The many tree branches hanging over the trail require you to be attentive through this section of the trail. Be sure to wear a long-sleeved shirt and a good hat.

When you reach the Crest Trail No. 130, you will be looking down on Albuquerque. Turn right and follow the trail as it curves to the north, allowing great views of I-40 heading east. The route along the crest passes through small scrub oaks, guaranteeing beautiful vistas in every direction, including views of the Sangre de Cristo Mountains to the northeast. You are also exposed to wind, sun, and thunderstorms on the crest, so plan for inclement weather and dress accordingly.

Follow the Crest Trail 1.3 miles until reaching a four-way intersection. Take the Cienega Trail right (east) and head down the canyon, quickly leaving the scrub oak behind. The trail down is not as rocky as the one going up, but it is still not well maintained and you may again have to deal with some low branches. After 2 miles, you will meet the junction with Faulty Trail. Turn right (south) and follow Faulty for a little under 1.2 miles until reaching the junction with the horse bypass trail. Return to the parking area by the same way you got here. Faulty Trail and the bypass trail are multiuse trails, so be prepared to encounter mountain bikers as well as hikers. Once in the wilderness, the trails are open to hikers and horseback riders only.

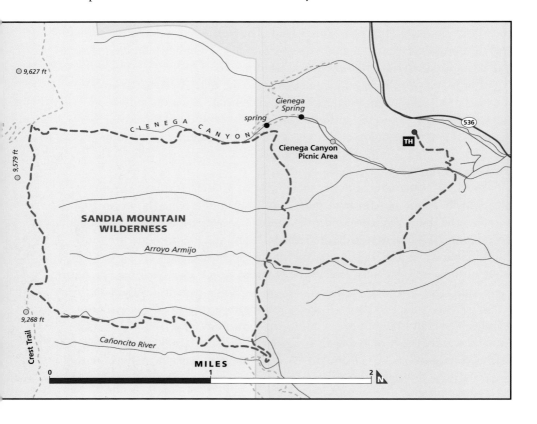

# South Crest Trail 59

Sandia Mountain Wilderness,
Cibola National Forest, Sandia Ranger District

| | |
|---|---|
| 10.6 miles | **Round-Trip Distance** |
| 6,500–9,400 feet | **Elevation Range** |
| Strenuous | **Difficulty** |
| Late April through October | **Best Season** |
| Parking area for horse trailers | **Horse Facilities** |
| Travertine Falls, small spring on South Crest Trail | **Water** |
| Yes | **Shoes Needed** |
| Tijeras USGS 7.5-minute quad; USFS Sandia Mountain Wilderness | **Maps** |
| Gorgeous views, a small waterfall | **Special Attractions** |

## Directions to Trailhead

From Albuquerque, take I-40 east to the Tijeras exit. After exiting, turn left, traveling under the interstate, then right, taking the road into Canyon Estates. Follow this road for a little over 0.5 mile to the trailhead. There is an area for horse trailer parking and a $3 parking fee for using the trailhead.

This ride is almost entirely in the sun and can be extremely hot during the summer, but it is an extremely popular trailhead nonetheless. When we rode it on a weekday in mid-May, the parking lot was crowded with cars. Most of these people were en route to Travertine Falls, but we did run into some hikers on the South Crest Trail.

The trailhead starts next to the pay station. Follow South Crest Trail No. 130 as it climbs out of the parking area. After 0.4 mile, you come to the junction of Trail No. 130 and Travertine Falls. Follow Trail No. 130 as it loops around and crosses over the top of Travertine Falls. About 0.8 mile from the

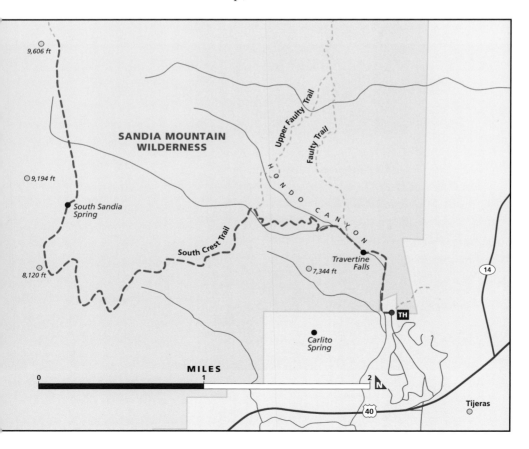

trailhead, the path intersects with Faulty Trail No. 195. You could use this trail to do a shorter loop if you wanted to, following it north until it connects with Upper Faulty Trail.

Continue on Trail No. 130 for another 1.2 miles, passing the junction with Upper Faulty Trail and CCC Trail No. 214. Turn left (south), staying on Trail No. 130 as it gradually switchbacks up the southern edge of the Sandia Mountains. As you climb, you will be rewarded with spectacular views of the Manzano Mountains to the south, the flatlands to the east, and even occasionally the Sangre de Cristo Mountains to the north. At 2.75 miles from the junction with Upper Faulty Trail, you come to a stock tank fed by a small spring. This will be a very welcome sight for your horses. Continue for another mile and you will be treated to wonderful views of Albuquerque far below. Turn around when ready and return to the trailhead by the same route.

# 60 Albuquerque Trail

Manzano Mountain Wilderness,
Cibola National Forest, Mountainair Ranger District

| | |
|---|---|
| **Round-Trip Distance** | 6.7 miles |
| **Elevation Range** | 7,450–8,850 feet |
| **Difficulty** | Easy |
| **Best Season** | May through October |
| **Horse Facilities** | Corrals at trailhead |
| **Water** | Small stream at trailhead (may be flowing), small stock tank in Fourth of July Canyon |
| **Shoes Needed** | Yes |
| **Maps** | Bosque Peak USGS 7.5-minute quad; USFS Manzano Mountain Wilderness |
| **Special Attractions** | Majestic views, great fall colors |

# Red Canyon

## 62

Manzano Mountain Wilderness,
Cibola National Forest, Mountainair Ranger District

| | |
|---|---|
| 7 miles | **Round-Trip Distance** |
| 7,900–9,730 feet | **Elevation Range** |
| Moderate | **Difficulty** |
| May through October | **Best Season** |
| Corrals at trailhead | **Horse Facilities** |
| Red Canyon, Spruce Spring | **Water** |
| Yes | **Shoes Needed** |
| Capilla Peak, Manzano Peak USGS 7.5-minute quads; USFS Manzano Mountain Wilderness | **Maps** |
| Views of the Rio Grande Valley, waterfalls, a lush green canyon | **Special Attractions** |

**Directions to Trailhead**

From Mountainair, go north for 13 miles on NM 55 until you reach Manzano. In Manzano, take NM 131 southwest for 3 miles until FR 253. There are signs for Red Canyon Campground. Stay on FR 253 and follow the signs to the horse facilities, which are adjacent to the trailhead. There is a $7-per-night fee for camping at Red Canyon Campground.

The trailhead for Spruce Spring Trail No. 189 is located conveniently next to the corral area, across from the first set of bathrooms. Trail No. 189 initially takes you north through aspen, ponderosa pine, Douglas fir, and spruce trees at a moderate grade on a rocky trail. At mile 2.6, you'll pass a Manzano Wilderness sign and are now officially in the wilderness area. About 0.5 mile later, you will see a side trail that leads to Spruce Spring, about 300 feet off the trail. Continue on Trail No. 189. Approximately 0.5 mile after the side trail for the spring, you'll meet the Crest Trail No. 170 in a saddle that forms a small meadow.

Turn left and follow this trail south as it begins to gain elevation. We rode the trail in the middle of May during an abnormally wet year and found 3- and 4-foot drifts of snow on this stretch that we had to lead the horses through. Trail No. 170 continues for 1.2 miles before intersecting with Red Canyon Trail No. 89. Before heading left (southwest) on Red Canyon Trail, it is worth taking a small detour to the right and up into the saddle through a break in the fence to see the Rio Grande Valley below. Our horses took advantage of the good grazing here while we took in the view.

In a short distance, Trail No. 89 meets up with a small stream. There are several stream crossings, and in the wet year that we rode it, the stream ran over the trail in a couple of places, so be sure to take a horse that is comfortable with water and stream crossings. The trail takes you past two little waterfalls and some beautiful cliffs. Trail No. 89 extends for 1.4 miles before reaching the wilderness boundary sign. The trailhead is another mile beyond that.

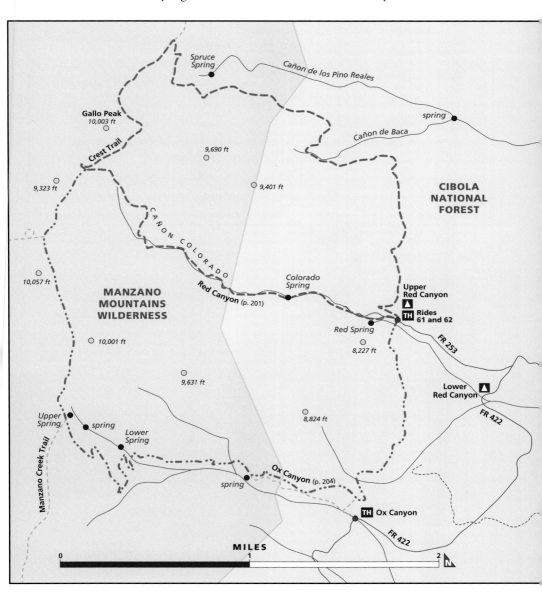

# 63 Ox Canyon

Manzano Mountain Wilderness,
Cibola National Forest, Mountainair Ranger District

| | |
|---|---|
| **Round-Trip Distance** | 7.75 miles |
| **Elevation Range** | 7,900–9,900 feet |
| **Difficulty** | Moderate to strenuous |
| **Best Season** | May through October |
| **Horse Facilities** | Corrals at trailhead |
| **Water** | Ox Canyon, Red Canyon |
| **Shoes Needed** | Yes |
| **Maps** | Capilla Peak, Manzano Peak USGS 7.5-minute quads; USFS Manzano Mountain Wilderness |
| **Special Attractions** | Sweeping views of the Rio Grande Valley, waterfalls, lush green canyons |

## Directions to Trailhead
Follow the directions to Red Canyon Campground (ride 62, p. 201).

Take Box Canyon Trail No. 99 south out of the hiker parking area. It will immediately cross a stream and pass through the gate, then gradually climb through scrub oak and ponderosa pine. In 1.4 miles, it intersects Ox Canyon Trail No. 190. Turn right, following Trail No. 190 west. In just under 0.5 mile, it crosses into the wilderness, becoming steep and rocky as it switchbacks up Ox Canyon. You will cross a small stream near Lower Ox Spring and continue toward Crest Trail No. 170 through a large area of aspen trees.

Five miles from the trailhead, the path intersects Trail No. 170. The junction is at a small saddle that provides a nice place to eat lunch while your horses rest. When you are ready, turn right onto Trail No. 170 and head north. When we rode the trail in mid-May, significant amounts of snow still lingered on the trail, though not as much as on the Red Canyon ride (ride 62, p. 201). The trail was also hard to follow in a couple of places. But later in the season, once all the snow melts and the trail gets used more heavily, it should not be hard to follow at all.

After 1 mile on Trail No. 170, you pass the junction for Salas Trail No. 184 on your left. Continue on Trail No. 170 for another 0.5 mile until meeting Red Canyon Trail No. 89 heading southeast down the canyon on your right. Before turning on the trail, it is worth taking the time to go left (west) and up into the saddle through a break in the fence. The views of the Rio Grande Valley below are lovely.

Trail No. 89 can be wet, with numerous stream crossings, so be sure you are riding a horse comfortable with those conditions (see ride 62, p. 203, for further description). Enjoy the two waterfalls and beautiful cliffs along the way. The trail continues for 1.4 miles before passing the wilderness boundary sign. The trailhead is located another mile after that.

## Trail Map
See page p. 203.

# Chapter Four

# Lincoln National Forest

Camp Wilderness Ridge

The Lincoln National Forest encompasses over 1.1 million acres of land and is divided into the Smokey Bear, Sacramento, and Guadalupe Ranger Districts, as well as two wilderness areas: the 48,873-acre White Mountain Wilderness and the 35,822-acre Capitan Mountains Wilderness.

## White Mountain Wilderness

This area is administered by the Smokey Bear Ranger District, which is named after the real Smokey Bear, a small black bear cub found singed and clinging to a charred tree after the 1950 Capitan Gap Wildfire. You can visit Smokey Bear Historical Park and Museum in the village of Capitan, where Smokey Bear is buried. Also nearby is Ruidoso Downs, home of the richest quarter horse race in the world.

The Smokey Bear Ranger District features two separate wilderness areas, White Mountain and Capitan Mountains. Together, they provide about 83,000 acres of wilderness, 49,000 of which are in the White Mountains. The Capitan

Mountains Wilderness is one of the few mountain ranges that run east–west, making it unique in southern New Mexico. This range is visible from the Texas state line on clear days and is generally the first range that visitors from the east see upon entering New Mexico.

In 2004, much of the Capitan Mountains Wilderness was burned in a wildfire, and currently the Forest Service is recommending White Mountain Wilderness as the better recreational option. As with other wilderness areas, travel is limited to foot or horseback.

### Camping and Horse Facilities

Camping and horse corrals are available at the Argentina/Bonito trailhead. Because it is indicated as a trailhead and not a campground, it is easy to miss, but there are pit toilets and a stream running nearby. You will pass Southfork Campground on the way to the Argentina/Bonito trailhead. Horses are not allowed in this campground, so continue on FR 107 past Southfork until the road dead-ends. The trailhead is found at the end of this road.

## Sacramento Ranger District

The Sacramento Ranger District is home to Cloudcroft, a 19th-century resort town popular with people looking to escape the plains' summer heat. To reach Cloudcroft from Alamogordo, the Alamogordo–Sacramento Mountain Railroad climbed over 5,000 feet in 26 miles. At the time it was built, the railroad was the highest standard-gauge rail in the world, requiring 58 wooden trestles, the longest of which was called the "S" Trestle. It had a length of 338 feet and a height of 60 feet and was formed as a double curve.

Many of the trails in the Sacramento Ranger District follow old railroad grades through mixed-conifer forest. Toward the southern part of the ranger district, you can still find some stands of old-growth forest that have never been logged. Access into the district can be gained through NM 6563, also called the Sunspot Highway.

### Camping and Horse Facilities

There are many improved campsites in the Sacramento Ranger District, although horses are not allowed in any of them. Fortunately, dispersed camping with your horses is available in plenty of areas. Another option is to stay at the shipping pens 2 miles from Bluff Springs (see ride 67, p. 217). Cloudcroft is the closest place for services such as gas, food, and water, and drinking water is also available at the Trestle Recreation Area. When we were there in the spring, the bathroom sinks were on, but the outside water was still turned off.)

# Guadalupe Ranger District

The Guadalupe Ranger District covers 285,000 acres and is the farthest south of the three. Sitting on the border of New Mexico and Texas, it butts up against Guadalupe Mountains National Park to the south and Carlsbad Caverns National Park along the eastern boundary. The Guadalupe Mountains rise sharply out of the desert to peaks over 7,000 feet in elevation. Most of the trails in this part of the national forest are up on ridgelines since the canyons are so rugged. You must be extremely alert for thunderstorms rolling in, especially during the late summer. Snow does fall in the winter but will generally melt fairly quickly. Springtime can bring strong winds, while summer brings extreme heat, even at 7,000 feet. Many people consider fall the best time to visit the Guadalupe Mountains, though with a little planning, any time of year is a great time to ride.

There is very little water in the Guadalupe Mountains, so your trip will also need to be planned around where you can get water or how much you can carry in your trailer.

If you are interested in pack trips, this is a great area to do them in—just make sure you talk to a ranger before you go and find out where you will be able to get water.

## Camping and Horse Facilities

There are no official campgrounds in this area, but there are locations for dispersed camping off of FR 540. Two places that offer dispersed camping also have livestock water nearby (see ride 70, p. 226).

A view of Big Canyon

## Other Areas

### La Cueva Non-Motorized Trail System

The La Cueva Non-Motorized Trail System is administered by the BLM and covers more than 2,000 acres in the foothills of the Guadalupe Mountains and the Chihuahuan Desert. Its nearly 15 miles of maintained trails are open to hiking, horseback riding, and mountain biking. While we don't include a route from this area in the book, it's a great place to ride and worth exploring.

The trailhead and parking area are close to the Carlsbad city limits. To get there, take NM 285 through town to Lea Street and turn right (west). At Standpipe Drive, turn left (south) and continue 3 miles to the gravel access road for La Cueva. This road is unmarked, so watch closely. Turn right and go approximately 0.3 mile to the trailhead and parking area on the left.

Although the trails are closed to motorized vehicles, a number of two-track four-wheel-drive roads crisscross the area, so you might still see some trucks or ATVs. We recommend contacting the BLM office and having them send you a map of the La Cueva Trail System so that you can get a sense for the routes before you arrive.

The trails can be rocky and sometimes hard to follow. In addition, there is no water available and it can be very hot, especially in the summer. Make sure you carry plenty of water for yourself and that you have enough water for your horses back at the trailer. We rode this area in early May and it was very pretty, with many of the cacti blooming. However, we arrived later in the day and were only able to do one short loop before Beamer lost his shoe (it was almost ready to come off—the trails aren't that rocky), so we weren't able to explore as much as we wanted to. But there are endless possibilities here, and you should get a copy of the map from the BLM and explore them on your own.

# Rides

| | | | |
|---|---|---|---|
| **64** Turkey Canyon | 210 | **68** Rim Trail | 220 |
| **65** Argentina Peak | 213 | **69** Rim Trail–Sunspot | 223 |
| **66** Big Bonito–Aspen Canyon | 215 | **70** Camp Wilderness Ridge | 226 |
| **67** Bluff Springs– | | **71** Big Canyon | 229 |
| Willie White Canyon | 217 | **72** Lonesome Ridge | 231 |

# 64 Turkey Canyon

## White Mountain Wilderness, Lincoln National Forest, Smokey Bear Ranger District

| | |
|---|---|
| **Round-Trip Distance** | 7 miles |
| **Elevation Range** | 7,750–9,150 feet |
| **Difficulty** | Moderate |
| **Best Season** | May through October |
| **Horse Facilities** | Corrals at trailhead |
| **Water** | Argentina Canyon, Turkey Canyon |
| **Shoes Needed** | Yes |
| **Maps** | Nogal Peak USGS 7.5-minute quad; USFS White Mountain Wilderness |
| **Special Attractions** | Spectacular views of Tularosa Basin and White Sands; El Malpais National Monument; lush, green canyons |

While we were camping here, a man was kicked by his mule and had to be airlifted out of the wilderness. Two days later, his mule still had not been found. It is important to remember that accidents can and do happen and you

## Directions to Trailhead

From Ruidoso, take NM 48 north 12 miles to the junction of NM 37. Turn left onto NM 37 and follow it for 1.3 miles until FR 107 turns left. This turn is signed for Bonito Lake. Follow FR 107 past the lake and the turnoff for Southfork Campground, at which point FR 107 turns into a gravel road. About 7.5 miles from NM 37, you pass by Bonito Riding Stables; the unnamed campground at the trailhead is a little less than 1 mile from the stables. Once you get to the campground, you will see the corrals on the left side of FR 107. There are four separate corrals, each of which is big enough for a couple of horses, as long as the horses get along. There are also a couple of vault toilets and trash receptacles.

Rides 64, 65, and 66 all start from the Argentina/Bonito trailhead, so you could combine some of the loops or ride farther on the Crest Trail for a longer ride.

should always let someone know where you are and when you plan on returning. It is also important to have some sort of wilderness first-aid knowledge if you are going to spend a lot of time in the mountains.

The Argentina Canyon Trail No. 39 begins on the north side of the camping area, across FR 107 from the last set of corrals. The trail climbs up Argentina Canyon above the stream. At around 0.75 mile, it crosses the stream and then shortly crosses again before climbing above the stream once more. The first mile of this ride passes by some huge trees and several rocky places on the trail. After about 1.5 miles, the trail returns to the stream and you come to the junction with Cut Across Trail No. 38, which heads off to your left. Stay straight on Argentina Canyon Trail.

The trail crosses the stream again, and then passes through a grove of aspen. About 0.7 mile after passing Cut Across Trail, Argentina Canyon Trail crests out, becoming muddy and rocky as water from Argentina Spring seeps through it. The large wooden fence here protects the spring. Clear Water Trail No. 42 goes right while Trail No. 39 veers left for another 0.2 mile before reaching Crest Trail No. 25 at mile 2.5. You could take Trail No. 42 if you wanted a shorter loop, but the views on Trail No. 25 are well worth the effort.

From the saddle where Trail No. 39 meets Trail No. 25, turn right, following it through a stand of Gambel oak. After coming out of the trees, the scenery opens up to the Tularosa Basin, with clear views of the town of Carrizozo and the lava flow of El Malpais National Monument.

Follow Trail No. 25 for approximately 1.15 miles until it meets up with Trail No. 42 again. The USFS map, along with many other topographic maps, shows a trail breaking off to the right of Trail No. 42, heading west down Turkey Canyon. However, we were unable to find this trail and continued along the Crest Trail until coming to Turkey Spring, marked by another fenced-off area and a sign for Turkey Canyon Trail No. 40. Turn right, heading downhill on the rocky and muddy trail. The beginning of Trail No. 40 is somewhat steep but will soon level out and continue down the canyon at a more gradual decline.

Continue down the canyon. At one point, the trail splits, with one section staying next to the stream and the other heading up. These shortly reconnect. About 1.33 miles down Turkey Canyon, you pass an old mine shaft. Remember that it is dangerous to enter the old mines. After another 0.75 mile, the trail takes you through a gate and then passes the sign for White Mountain Wilderness. Continue 0.5 mile until you meet FR 107. Turn right (southwest) onto FR 107 and follow it for 0.6 mile back to the corrals.

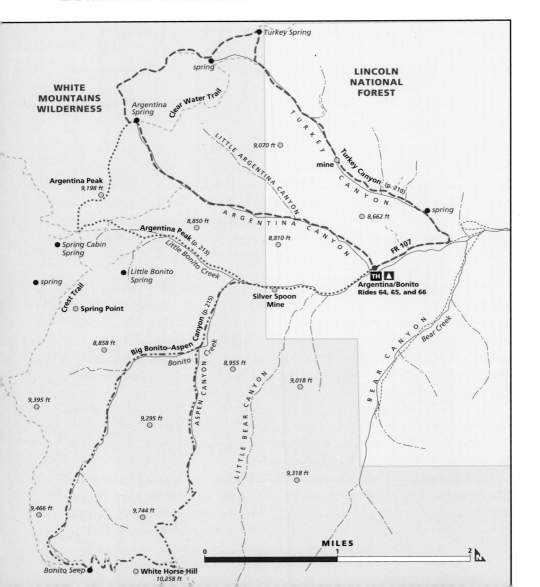

# Argentina Peak

## 65

White Mountain Wilderness, Lincoln
National Forest, Smokey Bear Ranger District

| | |
|---|---|
| 6 miles | **Round-Trip Distance** |
| 7,800–9,100 feet | **Elevation Range** |
| Moderate | **Difficulty** |
| May through October | **Best Season** |
| Corrals at trailhead | **Horse Facilities** |
| Bonito Creek, Argentina Canyon | **Water** |
| Yes | **Shoes Needed** |
| Nogal Peak USGS 7.5-minute quad; USFS White Mountain Wilderness | **Maps** |
| Spectacular views of Tularosa Basin and El Malpais National Monument | **Special Attractions** |

### Directions to Trailhead

Follow the directions to the Argentina/Bonito trailhead (ride 64, p. 210).

This ride showcases the beauty of the White Mountain Wilderness, with stunning views of some of its most impressive features. Big Bonito Trail No. 36 is located at the western end of the camping area. Cross the stream coming out of Argentina Canyon and enter the wilderness. The trail soon crosses Bonito Creek, one of the many crossings on this ride. On the left side of the trail is a small cave/mining shaft. Remember that it is dangerous and illegal to enter abandoned mines.

The trail climbs the canyon floor, following Bonito Creek. After 0.75 mile, it passes the opening to the Silver Spoon Mine and in a short distance comes to the junction of Little Bonito Trail No. 37. Turn right onto Little Bonito Trail. At just under 2 miles, a faint trail follows the stream while Trail No. 37 veers right, away from the stream. Stay on Trail No. 37 past the junction with the Cut Across Trail No. 38. Soon, you come to a five-way intersection on a beautiful saddle. Turn right, following Crest Trail No. 25.

This trail is steep and rocky for the first 0.15 mile as it climbs to a small meadow. Enjoy the views to the south, including White Horse Hill. At approximately 2.7 miles, the trail reaches a meadow on the east side of Argentina Peak, offering stunning views of the White Mountain Wilderness, including Nogal Peak to the north. The trail follows the crest of the ridge for the next 0.7 mile until reaching an intersection with Argentina Canyon Trail No. 39. If you want to extend this ride by traveling farther on the Crest Trail, see ride 64 (p. 210). Make sure you enjoy the views of the Tularosa Basin and the lava flow of El Malpais National Monument.

Turn right on Trail No. 39, following it downhill for 0.1 mile. You will see a large wooden enclosure protecting the spring and here will meet the Clear Water Trail No. 42. Turn right, following Trail No. 39 down Argentina Canyon. The first part of the trail is muddy, as part of the spring seeps down the trail. Trail No. 39 continues down the canyon for approximately the next 2.5 miles until you leave the wilderness and come back to the trailhead where you started.

## Trail Map

See page p. 212.

# Big Bonito–
# Aspen Canyon

White Mountain Wilderness, Lincoln
National Forest, Smokey Bear Ranger District

# 66

| | |
|---|---|
| 9.6 miles | **Round-Trip Distance** |
| 7,800–10,000 feet | **Elevation Range** |
| Moderate | **Difficulty** |
| May through October | **Best Season** |
| Corrals at trailhead | **Horse Facilities** |
| Bonito Creek, Aspen Canyon | **Water** |
| Yes | **Shoes Needed** |
| Nogal Peak USGS 7.5-minute quad; USFS White Mountain Wilderness | **Maps** |
| Spectacular views; lush, green canyons, subalpine meadows | **Special Attractions** |

| **Directions to Trailhead** |

Follow the directions to the Argentina/Bonito trailhead (ride 64, p. 210).

This ride, like others in the region, is distinguished by great views of Nogal Peak and the White Mountain Wilderness. Three rides in this book start from the Argentina/Bonito trailhead—should you wish to make any one of them longer, simply combine some of the loops or ride on the Crest Trail farther than directed.

Start out on the Big Bonito Trail No. 36, located at the western end of the camping area (see ride 65, p. 213, for further description). After 1 mile, the Big Bonito Trail intersects with the Little Bonito Trail No. 37. Turn left, staying on Trail No. 36 as it heads south. In another 0.7 mile, you come to the junction with Aspen Canyon Trail No. 35. Turn left and begin to climb up Aspen Canyon. The trail parallels a small stream. As you climb, the trees gradually turn to aspen until you leave the trees behind and begin to ascend switchbacks through the grasslands. You will be able to see Nogal Peak to the north and the Capitan Range to the east.

The trail crests out near mile 3 and veers to the right, climbing slightly to the next ridge, where you come to a four-way trail junction. Three Rivers Canyon Trail No. 44 goes straight south while the Crest Trail No. 25 goes to the right and left. Turn right (west) on the Crest Trail, heading toward White Horse Hill. During the summer when the grass is growing, the trail could become hard to follow. Plan for potential snow, too, if you are riding in the spring: We rode the trail in the middle of May and had to turn around by White Horse Hill due to a large snowfield on the north side.

If the trail is open, continue around the north side of White Horse Hill until the trail switchbacks down to Bonito Seep at a little under 5 miles. At this point, you meet Big Bonito Trail. Turn right, heading down the canyon, following Bonito Creek. Continue on this trail for approximately 2 miles until you meet up with Aspen Canyon Trail. Turn left and continue back to the trailhead following Trail No. 36.

## Trail Map

See page p. 212.

# Bluff Springs–Willie White Canyon

## 67

Lincoln National Forest, Sacramento Ranger District

| | |
|---|---|
| 8.4 miles | **Round-Trip Distance** |
| 8,080–9,370 feet | **Elevation Range** |
| Easy | **Difficulty** |
| May through October | **Best Season** |
| Set of shipping pens at trailhead | **Horse Facilities** |
| Water Canyon, small springs along the way | **Water** |
| Yes | **Shoes Needed** |
| Bluff Springs, Sacramento Peak USGS 7.5-minute quads | **Maps** |
| Historic railroad grades, dense ponderosa pine and aspen forest | **Special Attractions** |

## Directions to Trailhead

From the west edge of Cloudcroft, turn off of US 82 south onto NM 130. Follow NM 130 for two miles and turn right (south) onto NM 6563, also called the Sunspot Highway. In just under 9 miles, turn left (east) onto FR 164, also known as CR C17, and proceed for 2 miles until you reach a set of shipping pens. This would be the most convenient place to overnight your horses if you are camping. You should check with the ranger first, though, in case the Forest Service or lessees are planning to use them. In early May, when we were in this area, water was flowing out of Water Canyon just past the pens and we were able to water the horses there. Make sure that you double-check with the ranger before you count on that water, however. If you don't want to stay at the pens or if they are being used, several good dispersed camping spots are available just off the road up Water Canyon.

This ride winds its way through many beautiful canyons as it follows old railroad grades, left over from the region's historic mining and logging days. From the shipping pens, continue following FR 164 east, staying off to the side of the road. Bluff Springs is very popular in the summer and there could be considerable traffic. After passing the ruins of an old cabin at 0.66 mile, you need to go through a small piece of private property, marked by a gate next to the cattle guard. Be sure that you shut the gate after going through. For the next 0.5 mile, you should stay on the road, watching for traffic. Go through another gate back onto national forest land at 1.3 miles.

In approximately another 0.5 mile, you come to the Bluff Springs parking area, featuring a small lot, vault toilets, and a large, flat area that looks like it once was a campsite for horses and riders. Cross the dry streambed by the footbridge and take Trail No. 112 off to your left. The trail to your right goes to the top of the bluff. At the beginning of the trail, you will see a large sign with a map of the loop you are about to ride.

About 2.1 miles from the start of this ride, the trail goes around the ruins of an old train trestle and almost immediately comes to a gate. Go through and continue up the old railroad grade for another 0.2 mile until Trail No. 112

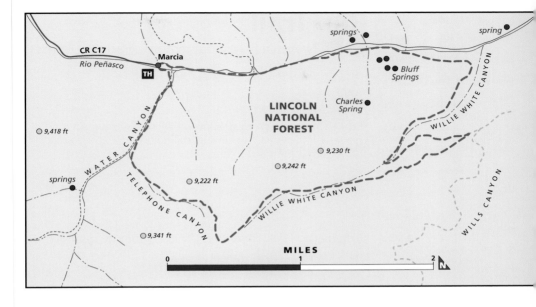

intersects Trail No. 113. Trail No. 113 is open to motorized vehicles. Though we did not see any vehicles while we were riding, we did see tracks.

At this point, you follow Trail No. 113, which continues along the old railroad grade through a forest of mixed conifers. In late spring and summer, wildflowers will mix with the green meadow grass to create a rainbow of beautiful colors. The colors are also excellent in the fall when the leaves of the maple and aspen trees change.

At 3.5 miles, the railroad grade crosses the floor of the canyon and swings hard to the left, going to the other side and then heading down the canyon. Another old grade continues up the canyon floor; explore that if you wish. In another 0.5 mile, Trail No. 113 intersects with Trail No. 5008, which switchbacks down into Wills Canyon. Some older maps have it labeled as Trail No. 9277. Make a sharp right, staying on Trail No. 113, and head up Willie White Canyon. In another mile, the trail leaves the railroad grade, crosses the canyon bottom, and continues up the canyon on the north side.

At this point, the trail begins to get a little rocky but is still manageable. At just under 6 miles, you come to the ridgetop overlooking Willie White Canyon and Telephone Canyon. An old logging road follows the crest, and Trail No. 5008 branches off left into Wills Canyon. Follow Trail No. 113 as it descends into Telephone Canyon. The trail drops quickly, losing 700 feet of elevation in a little over 1 mile. Continue on Trail No. 113 until it ends at FR 5009 (Water Canyon). Turn right (north) and follow the road to the shipping pens.

# 68 Rim Trail

Lincoln National Forest, Sacramento Ranger District

| | |
|---|---|
| **Round-Trip Distance** | 12 miles |
| **Elevation Range** | 8,360–9,300 feet |
| **Difficulty** | Easy to strenuous, depending on distance traveled |
| **Best Season** | May through October |
| **Horse Facilities** | No |
| **Water** | No |
| **Shoes Needed** | Yes |
| **Maps** | Sacramento Peak, High Rolls USGS 7.5-minute quads |
| **Special Attractions** | Views of Tularosa Basin, fall colors |

## Directions to Trailhead

From the western edge of Cloudcroft, turn off of US 82 south onto NM 130. Follow NM 130 for 2 miles and turn right onto NM 6563, also called the Sunspot Highway. The Slide Group Area is immediately off to your right, along with a gravel pullover area in which to park.

The 22-mile Rim Trail was the first trail to be designated as a National Recreation Trail in New Mexico. The trail is a combination of old Indian paths, railroad grades, and homestead trails tied together by some new sections built in the 1960s. Markers are placed every mile, although many have been damaged by vandals; if you keep your eyes out for them, they can help you keep track of where you are.

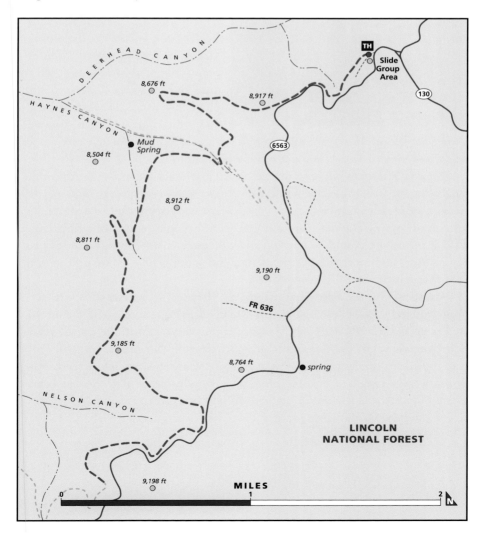

Pass through the gate to the right of the entrance to Slide Group Area. Take Trail No. 105 to the left. If you take it to the right, it will take you down to Deerhead Campground. The trail swings around to the south and leads you behind the group area. Around 0.75 mile, it comes close to the Sunspot Highway, then heads to the west and leads you out onto a long ridge. The trail along the ridge offers some of the best views during the first half of the Rim Trail. You can see the Tularosa Basin, including part of White Sands National Monument. Off to your right is Sierra Blanca, which, at 12,000 feet, is the highest peak in southern New Mexico. You will appreciate a long-sleeved shirt as the trail leads you through a tangle of Gambel oak, New Mexico locust, and oceanspray bushes.

Shortly after passing mile marker 2, the trail cuts across the bottom of a small canyon and in another 0.25 mile crosses an old logging road along the bottom of Haynes Canyon. This would be an interesting trail to explore. As you climb out of Haynes Canyon, you pass through an area of maple trees. In fall, the colors should be nothing short of spectacular. You will also start to notice more and more massive ponderosa and southwestern white pine as you pass through the mixed-confiner forest.

Continue on the Rim Trail (Trail No. 105) until you cross FR 636 at approximately 4.5 miles. Again, this is a good place to explore if the desire strikes you. Trail No. 105 is off to your right. As you continue up the trail, enjoy the views off to your right. At approximately 5.5 miles, you will see a trail signed for the Sunspot Highway going to your left. Just before the 6-mile point, a large tangle of deadfall blocked our path. Hopefully, this has been cleared by the time you are riding here. When ready, turn around and return to the trailhead by the same route.

# Rim Trail–Sunspot

# 69

Lincoln National Forest, Sacramento Ranger District

| | |
|---:|:---|
| 4 miles | **Round-Trip Distance** |
| 9,000–9,500 feet | **Elevation Range** |
| Moderate | **Difficulty** |
| May through October | **Best Season** |
| No | **Horse Facilities** |
| No | **Water** |
| Yes | **Shoes Needed** |
| Sacramento Peak USGS 7.5-minute quad | **Maps** |
| Dense, old-growth forest; views of Tularosa Basin | **Special Attractions** |

## Directions to Trailhead

From the western edge of Cloudcroft, turn off of US 82 south onto NM 130. Follow 130 for 2 miles and turn right onto NM 6563, also called the Sunspot Highway. Continue on this road for 12 miles until you see the sign for Cathey Canyon Vista. Turn right into the parking lot. The trailhead will be off to your right and the return trail off to your left. Note that you will pass the turnoff for Bluff Springs approximately 9 miles after turning onto the Sunspot Highway. This is a good area to spend the night if you are camping (see ride 67, p. 217).

This short loop makes for a varied, interesting ride as it passes through dense forest and changes elevation. Pull into the parking lot for the Cathey Canyon Vista. This is a big pull-in area and should have enough room for a horse trailer. You will see a sign for Trail No. 105 and FR 5011. Take this road as it heads north away from the parking area. Be sure to check out the scenic vista off to the left as you start.

At about 0.3 mile, Trail No. 105 branches off to the left. When we rode this trail in the middle of May, some small patches of snow still remained on

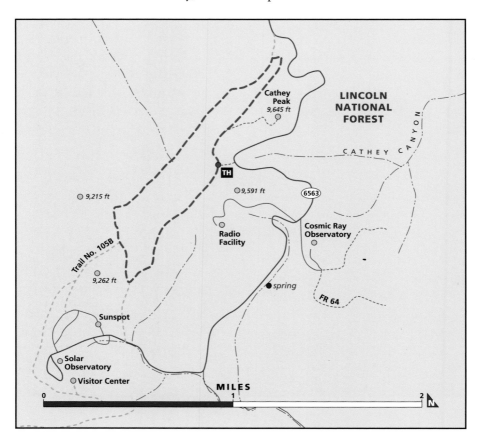

the ground. You will see an old logging road continuing straight. Make sure you take Trail No. 105 as it branches off to the left and heads slightly downhill. Soon you will see the Sunspot Highway off to your right, and then the trail curves left away from the highway. Trail No. 105 continues until it comes to a T intersection at a fence. Trail No. 105 goes right, following the fence, while Trail No. 105A turns left, also staying along the fence line. If you take Trail No. 105, it very shortly comes to a walk-through fence and runs next to the Sunspot Highway for a short distance. Take Trail No. 105A and follow it south as it travels through an area of old-growth mixed-conifer forest that has never been logged. Watch out for barbwire, as the old fence the trail follows is on the ground in many places.

The trail drops down for a short distance before it levels out again. There are a few downed trees on the trail that we had to find our way around and a couple of spots between the trees and the old fence where it might be a tight squeeze for your horse. The trail passes by a huge downed tree and then starts to climb again, still along the old fence line.

Soon the trail leaves the fence and you will see a trail marker signed for Trail Nos. 105A and 105B. Trail No. 105A goes straight, while Trail No. 105B goes right. Continue on Trail No. 105A as it slowly climbs up the hill. As you reach the top and a small meadow, you will see a sign for Trail No. 105. If you follow Trail No. 105 right, it takes you to the Sunspot Highway; left takes you back to your truck. You will pass an old logging road that forks off to your left and then, shortly after, one that branches off to the right. Trail No. 105 should be easy to stay on in both cases. Follow Trail No. 105 until you reach the parking lot for the Cathey Canyon Vista. This ride could easily be made longer by taking the Trail No. 105B loop or continuing on Trail No. 105 either north or south.

# 70 Camp Wilderness Ridge
## Lincoln National Forest, Guadalupe Ranger District

| | |
|---|---|
| **Round-Trip Distance** | 8 miles |
| **Elevation Range** | 7,000–7,400 feet |
| **Difficulty** | Strenuous |
| **Best Season** | Year-round |
| **Horse Facilities** | No |
| **Water** | Livestock tank at trailhead |
| **Shoes Needed** | Yes |
| **Maps** | El Paso Gap NM TX USGS 7.5-minute quad |
| **Special Attractions** | Spectacular views, ruins of an old cabin |

## Directions to Trailhead

From Carlsbad, take US 285 north for about 12 miles. Turn left (west) onto NM 137. You'll pass by the turnoff for Sitting Bull Falls after 24 miles. About 11 miles farther is the Guadalupe National Forest Administrative Center. This is the last available place to obtain potable water. It is also a good idea to stop here and tell the rangers where you plan on camping and/or riding.

About 3 more miles west, you will pass the Queen General Store, which has basic supplies and great hamburgers, if it is open. Several miles past the Queen store, turn left onto FR 540, a well-marked and well-maintained all-weather gravel road. After 0.5 mile, bear right (staying on the main gravel road) and continue south along FR 540. Enjoy the numerous scenic vistas along this road.

After 12 miles, the road passes a well-maintained turnaround area. Most hikers park here. This is also where you can start on the trail to Lonesome Ridge (see ride 72, p. 231). Stay on FR 540, crossing a cattle guard. There is a stock tank here and a set of branding pens. You would need to check with the rangers to see if you are allowed to camp here. The pens are used by the lessees, who run cattle on this part of the national forest.

If you follow FR 540 for an additional 1.3 miles, you will come to a big open parking area with an old oil derrick that is now a water pump. A number of nice camping areas line FR 540 before you get to the oil derrick, but they have no water close by. There is a livestock watering tank in the vicinity. If you decide to camp here, you must camp far enough away from the tank that you will not disturb any cattle that might come to water here. The last 1.3 miles of FR 540 are rough but passable with a truck and horse trailer.

This ride takes you within miles of the Texas border, offering gorgeous views of several dramatic canyons. From the oil derrick, follow FR 540 back the way you came for 1 mile. You will see Trail No. 201, an old Forest Service road, on your left. You may also see four-wheel-drive vehicles or ATVs on this trail. After 0.25 mile, you pass an old stock tank off to your left. Don't count on it having any water in it. Continue up the hill, staying to your left as you climb through a recent burn area.

About 1.8 miles from the start, Devils Den Trail No. 202 branches off to your right (east). Follow this trail down for 0.6 mile until you come to the ruins of an old cabin. The path is rough and rocky. After you get to the cabin, you should continue past it for another 0.1 mile to a spectacular lookout over Devils Den Canyon. After enjoying the view from the point, return to Trail No. 201 the same way you came to the cabin. Continue right (south) up Trail No. 201 for another 0.3 mile, at which point you come to the intersection of Camp Wilderness Ridge Trail No. 45 and North McKittrick Canyon Trail.

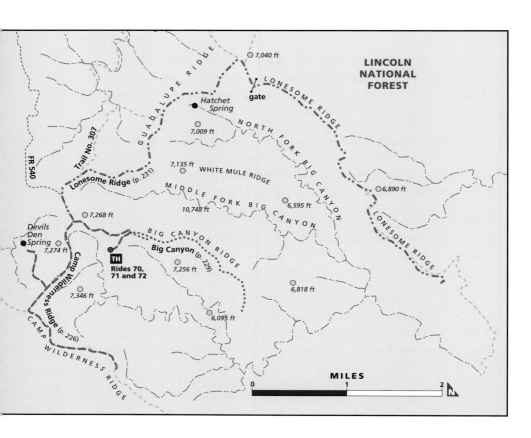

Turn left (southwest), following the Camp Wilderness Ridge Trail No. 45 for another 0.6 mile until you get to a stunning vista. At this point, you have ridden approximately 4 miles. Camp Wilderness Ridge Trail No. 45 stays on top of the ridge, giving you outstanding views of North McKittrick Canyon the entire time. We followed the trail for another 0.75 mile before turning around. The trail continues on to the edge of Lincoln National Forest and Guadalupe Mountains National Park in Texas. Return by the same route when ready.

# Big Canyon 71

Lincoln National Forest, Guadalupe Ranger District

| | |
|---|---|
| 4.25 miles | **Round-Trip Distance** |
| 7,000–7,250 feet | **Elevation Range** |
| Moderate | **Difficulty** |
| Year-round | **Best Season** |
| No | **Horse Facilities** |
| Livestock tank at trailhead | **Water** |
| Yes | **Shoes Needed** |
| El Paso Gap NM TX USGS 7.5-minute quad | **Maps** |
| Spectacular views | **Special Attractions** |

## Directions to Trailhead

Follow the directions for Camp Wilderness Ridge (ride 70, p. 226) to the camping area and trailhead on FR 540.

For almost the entire route, this ride rewards you with fantastic scenery and gorgeous views. From the oil derrick, go 0.3 mile to the intersection of FR 540 and FR 9553 on the right (east). FR 9553 is an old jeep trail that could have ATVs or four-wheel-drive vehicles on it. Take FR 9553 and follow it for 1 mile until it opens up on your left with a great view of Lonesome Ridge.

Continue up the path for 0.15 mile. At this point, the trail becomes less distinct as it goes to the right around a little hill. After another 0.25 mile, the trail becomes fainter and drops you down into a little valley, probably created when a large cave collapsed many, many years ago. It is a great place to tie up your horses, have lunch, and enjoy the view. The floor of Big Canyon lies only 1,800 feet below. On a clear day, you can see for over 130 miles. You could turn around and head back at this point, but it is worth it to follow the faint game trail to the southern tip of the ridge and enjoy those views also. Return to your trailer by the same route.

### Trail Map

See page p. 228.

# Lonesome Ridge

## Lincoln National Forest, Guadalupe Ranger District

**72**

| | |
|---|---|
| 16 miles, including 2 miles walking | **Round-Trip Distance** |
| 6,700–7,250 feet | **Elevation Range** |
| Strenuous | **Difficulty** |
| Year-round | **Best Season** |
| No | **Horse Facilities** |
| Livestock tank at trailhead; at cattle guard 1 mile from trailhead | **Water** |
| Yes | **Shoes Needed** |
| El Paso Gap NM TX, Gunsight Canyon NM TX USGS 7.5-minute quads | **Maps** |
| Spectacular views | **Special Attractions** |

## Directions to Trailhead

Follow the directions for Camp Wilderness Ridge (ride 70, p. 226) to the camping area and trailhead on FR 540.

This is a challenging route for both horse and rider, but it feels worth the effort once you are enjoying the views atop Lonesome Ridge. From the oil derrick, head back on FR 540 for 1.3 miles to the gravel turnaround. When you go through the gate by the cattle guard, you pass by the last water available on this ride. Once at the gravel turnaround, take Trail No. 201, a four-wheel-drive road off to your right. The trail is extremely rocky in places. In about 0.3 mile, Trail No. 201 intersects with Trail No. 307. You will want to stay on Trail No. 201, which is also signed for Lonesome Ridge Trail No. 56. Follow the trail as it continues along the ridgetop, with numerous inclines and declines. After approximately 3.3 miles, Lonesome Ridge comes into view.

At mile 4.25, you arrive at a four-way intersection; turn right (south) onto Lonesome Ridge Trail No. 56, going left through a gate in 0.35 mile. Continue to follow the road across the saddle, enjoying the views of Big Canyon on your right and Black River Canyon on your left. The four-wheel-drive road (you would need to be an expert driver to have gotten this far) ends and becomes a trail open only to non-motorized travel 0.7 mile after the gate.

At this point, the trail becomes narrow, steep, rocky, and sometimes hard to follow. You should be an expert rider with a very solid trail horse to continue any farther. If you do continue, don't be afraid to get off and lead your horse through this section. It is easier for him to scramble over rocks with you off his back, plus it allows you to stretch your legs.

The trail skirts the edge of a limestone bowl overlooking Black River Canyon. This would be a place where you would want to be able to dismount from either side if you had to. After topping back out on the ridge, continue to follow the trail. At about mile 6, the trail becomes hard to see and it is easy to lose track of it. If you do lose the trail, head to your right (west) toward the little point overlooking Big Canyon. From there, you should be able to see the trail down the hill to your left (west).

The trail stays on the side of the drainage, not quite getting up on top of the ridge. About 6.5 miles after you start, you should find yourself in a saddle with Big Canyon straight down on your right. Follow the steep, rocky trail another 0.2 mile up before you come to the top of Lonesome Ridge. From here, we were able to follow the trail a little farther and rode down into a depression with some small trees. We tied our horses to one of the trees and enjoyed lunch with our feet hanging over the edge into Big Canyon. We saw a herd of bighorn sheep scrambling on the rocks below.

After lunch, we left our horses tied up and walked the last 1.2 miles to the edge of Lonesome Ridge. We would advise against trying to ride your horse to the point: The trail is extremely rocky with numerous up and downs and you have already asked a lot of him. We do recommend that you make it, however, since the views are outstanding and stretch for over 130 miles on a clear day. Take some pictures and walk back to your horse. Return to the trailer by the same route.

## Trail Map

See page p. 228.

# Chapter Five

# Gila National Forest

Sawmill Canyon

At 3.3 million acres, the Gila is the largest national forest in New Mexico. The elevation in this area ranges from 4,000 feet all the way to 11,000, making the Gila one of the most ecologically and geologically diverse places in the state. It boasts deep canyons, broad meadows, high mountain peaks, and rugged desert country, and hosts four of the six life zones and a wide variety of flora and fauna. There are 360 miles of streams and rivers as well as five lakes, many stocked with native trout. Over 1,500 miles of trails offer an unlimited amount of exploring.

The Gila encompasses so many trails and so much land that it would be possible to write an entire book about horseback riding in this area alone. For the purposes of this book, we chose rides that were close to corrals and more popular among horseback riders. If you are interested in the Gila beyond a handful of day trips, we urge you to explore further. As we were researching this area for the book, we were planning future trips with car shuttles and pack horses and daydreaming of the numerous possibilities.

Three wilderness areas—the Gila, the Aldo Leopold and the Blue Range—fall within the jurisdiction of Gila National Forest, which is administered by the Black Range, Glenwood, Wilderness, Reserve, Quemado, and Silver City Ranger Districts. There also is an information desk in Silver City and a visitor center at the Gila Cliff Dwellings National Monument.

## Gila Wilderness

Under the leadership of Aldo Leopold, the famous conservationist, the Gila Wilderness was established in 1924 as the first wilderness in the country. Leopold became familiar with the area around 1910 during his time as a ranger, when he came to appreciate the untouched splendor of the area and later strove to preserve it for future generations. The renowned Gila Cliff Dwellings National Monument is located here, and recreation opportunities include hiking, horseback riding, mountain biking, four-wheel-driving, skiing, snowshoeing, and snowmobiling. Remember, though, that no mechanized equipment is allowed in any of the designated wilderness areas.

### Camping and Horse Facilities

Scorpion Campground in the Gila Cliff Dwellings National Monument does not allow horses, but two different sets of corrals are found before the campground on NM 15. Woody's Corral is on the left side of the road, and TJ Corral is located a little farther down on the right. The year we were there, major flooding had caused damage to the water lines at TJ Corral. Because of this, all the horseback riders were crowded into Woody's and we had TJ to ourselves, but we had to haul water. Normally, however, both sets of corrals have water.

Be sure to check out Gila Cliff Dwellings National Monument. A trail about 1 mile long leads you through the cliff dwellings. Horses are not allowed in this area, we recommend leaving your horse in one of the corrals and exploring on foot. The self-guided tour costs $3 per person. Also there are wonderful hot springs along the Gila River in the town of Gila Hot Springs. They also cost $3 per person. After riding, we relished every minute of that hot water on our aching muscles.

Willow Creek Campground (see ride 76, p. 245) also does not allow horses. However, you can camp with horses at the trailhead on your way into and out of the wilderness, meaning for one or two nights. When you first pull into the area surrounding the trailhead, look to the right for an open grassy area that's good for an electric fence. Also, if you cross the stream and drive closer to the actual trailhead, you can find an open area there that is also good for camping.

Dipping Vat Campground at Snow Lake does not allow horses either, but dispersed camping is allowed outside of the recreation area. Also, about 4 miles up the road from Dipping Vat is Aeroplane Mesa Campground, which has a set of four corrals. No water is available here, but there is a stock tank right down the road, or you could haul water from Dipping Vat.

## Quemado Ranger District

This area has a rich history, with the Mogollon and Apache Indians as well as Mexicans and Spaniards contributing to its legacy. Some of the more famous names to call this region home were Chief Geronimo, Chief Loco, Mangas Coloradas and Butch Cassidy. As you ride, keep an eye out for ruins of old cabins and stone walls. You may also see some arrowheads and pottery shards if you look close enough, but keep in mind that federal law prohibits removing any such artifacts. Literature on the history of the Gila is always available in the surrounding ranger stations and visitor center.

### Camping and Horse Facilities

The trails we describe in this region are accessible from two camping areas. Valle Tio Vinces Campground has two sets of corrals and four campsites. There are toilets at the campground but no running water, though the Valle Tio Vinces Spring is across the road and a little to the north of the corrals. Armijo Spring Campground does not allow horses in the campground, but dispersed camping is allowed in the surrounding areas. Water is available from the Armijo Spring. Keep in mind, however, that camping is not allowed within 300 feet of the spring.

Quemado Lake is one of the popular recreation sites in this area. While it may seem like a wonderful place to camp and ride, the restrictions and lack of trails do not make it an ideal horseback riding area.

# Rides

73 West Fork Gila River ............ 237
74 EE Canyon ......................... 240
75 Middle Fork Gila River ......... 242
76 Iron Creek Mesa ................. 245
77 Snow Canyon .................... 248

78 Aeroplane Mesa ................. 251
79 Valle Tio Vinces ................. 254
80 Mangas Lookout Tower ....... 257
81 Sawmill Canyon ................. 259
82 Armijo Spring .................... 261

# West Fork Gila River

## 73

### Gila Wilderness, Gila National Forest, Wilderness Ranger District

| | |
|---|---|
| 8.2 miles | **Round-Trip Distance** |
| 5,700–5,825 feet | **Elevation Range** |
| Moderate | **Difficulty** |
| May through November | **Best Season** |
| Corrals at trailhead | **Horse Facilities** |
| At corrals and West Fork Gila River | **Water** |
| Yes | **Shoes Needed** |
| Gila Hot Springs, Little Turkey Park USGS 7.5-minute quads; USFS Gila Wilderness | **Maps** |
| West Fork Gila River, cave dwellings | **Special Attractions** |

This ride follows the West Fork of the Gila River past some breathtaking cliffs and an ancient cliff dwelling, making it a great trail to get acquainted with the region around the Gila Cliff Dwellings National Monument. Take Trail No. 729 leading out of TJ Corral. In 0.25 mile, you pass the first trail junction; from here, continue straight on Trail No. 151. This section of the ride winds around the hills and drainages above the national monument and brings you down on the back side of the park. This is the only way you can get here, because horses are not allowed in the park.

There are two gates to pass through, though when we were here, only the first one was closed. After you pass through the second gate, you come to a second trail junction at mile 2. The trail to the left leads to the cliff dwellings and is closed to horses. Bear right and cross the river. The trail heads up onto the bench above the river. Shortly after this is the third trail junction. Turning left would take you up EE Canyon (see ride 74, p. 240). Instead, continue straight at this junction and begin the gradual descent into the river canyon. The river and surrounding foliage offer a welcome relief from the heat that you probably experienced in the first 2 miles of this ride. The cliffs tower above in shades of gray, brown, and orange, tapering to fantastic peaks. You are likely to see many raptors circling the cliffs in search of food, or maybe a heron looking for a good branch to land on.

For the next 2 miles, you follow the river, crossing a few more times. Around mile 3.4, right after crossing the river, the trail comes to a junction with Trail No. 28. Go left, staying on Trail No. 151 along the river. Just after mile 4, a

## Directions to Trailhead

From Silver City, take NM 15 north. Stay on NM 15 for 42 miles. This road is paved, although steep and winding, and you should allow at least two hours to reach the corrals. The road is not recommended for trailers over 20 feet, though we did fine with our 20-foot trailer. Be careful and watch for other traffic. After 42 miles, turn left just before the visitor center, staying on NM 15. Woody's Corral is 0.5 mile farther, with TJ Corral another 0.25 mile beyond that, just past the West Fork of the Gila River. Both corrals have water available, although when we were here, the water at TJ was turned off due to damage caused by a spring flood. Woody's Corral is a popular starting place for pack trips into the Gila Wilderness. Along with the four large corrals are numerous hitching rails and a generous area for trailer parking. TJ Corral also has four large corrals, but no hitching rails and room for only a couple of trailers to park.

large cave is visible in the cliff wall in front of you. Cross the river and you will find a nice little camping area or picnic spot. Just to the left of the cave is a dwelling set into a smaller cave. The rangers ask that people not attempt to enter the dwelling or climb on the surrounding hillside, as foot traffic creates erosion that could be damaging to the structure of the dwelling. However, the view from the river is wonderful. Return to the corrals by the same route.

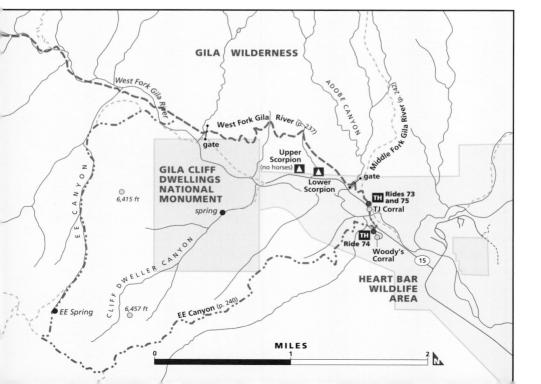

# 74 EE Canyon

Gila Wilderness, Gila National Forest,
Wilderness Ranger District

| | |
|---|---|
| **Round-Trip Distance** | 8.2 miles |
| **Elevation Range** | 5,650–6,650 feet |
| **Difficulty** | Moderate |
| **Best Season** | May through November |
| **Horse Facilities** | Corrals at trailhead |
| **Water** | At corrals, West Fork Gila River |
| **Shoes Needed** | Yes |
| **Maps** | Little Turkey Park USGS 7.5-minute quad; USFS Gila Wilderness |
| **Special Attractions** | Great views of the Gila Wilderness |

**Directions to Trailhead**

Follow the directions to Woody's and TJ Corrals (ride 73, p. 237).

This pleasant loop is easily lengthened if you are looking for a longer ride. Follow Trail No. 160 out the back of Woody's Corral. The rocky trail winds up and around to the top of the hills beyond the campgrounds. For the first mile, you will be able to see the road and camping areas behind you, but they in no way detract from the scenery. The trail is rocky in areas but very nicely maintained and manageable. At mile 2.85, you come to the first trail junction. Trail No. 160 continues down to Little Creek. If you want to make this a longer ride, you can ride down to the creek via Trail No. 160 and then loop back around to Trail No. 162. If you are happy with an 8-mile ride, then take the right fork onto Trail No. 162.

The views of the mountains open up to the right as you ride along the ridge. In another 0.6 mile, you come to the junction of Trail No. 162 and EE Canyon. The trail makes a sharp right turn here and continues down into the canyon. As you ride into the canyon, the foliage becomes denser and greener the closer you get to the river. Beautiful cliffs rise on both sides of the trail. Continue down the canyon until you come to a junction with Trail No. 151 approximately 5.7 miles from the trailhead. Go right and follow it to the crossing of the West Fork of the Gila River. This is the only place to water the horses and it was an easy place to cross when we were there. Earlier that spring, however, some major flooding in the area probably made this mellow crossing a raging river, so check with the local rangers before doing this ride.

Because horses are not allowed in the cliff dwellings area, the trail makes a wide loop around the park and then curves back around into the corrals. About 0.5 mile after turning onto Trail No. 151, you reach another junction. The horse trail passes through a gate and climbs up the ridge, traversing the edge of the hills above the campground roads. The path is narrow and rocky in some areas. You will be able to see the river as it parallels the road and will also have a nice view of the cliffs and mountains in the distance. About 0.25 mile before you get to the end of the ride, you pass through a gate, reaching another trail that leads up Little Bear Canyon to the left. Stay on the main trail until you come to TJ Corral. If this is where you are camped, then you're done. If you are staying at Woody's Corral, then it is a short jog down the road to the left.

## Trail Map

See page p. 238.

# 75 Middle Fork Gila River

Gila Wilderness, Gila National Forest,
Wilderness Ranger District

| | |
|---|---|
| **Round-Trip Distance** | 11 miles |
| **Elevation Range** | 5,650–6,370 feet |
| **Difficulty** | Strenuous |
| **Best Season** | May through November |
| **Horse Facilities** | Corrals at trailhead |
| **Water** | At corrals, Middle Fork Gila River |
| **Shoes Needed** | Yes |
| **Maps** | Little Turkey Park, Gila Hot Springs, Burnt Corral Canyon USGS 7.5-minute quads; USFS Gila Wilderness |
| **Special Attractions** | Little Bear Canyon, Middle Fork Gila River, soaring cliffs |

## Directions to Trailhead

Follow the directions to Woody's and TJ Corrals (ride 73, p. 237).

Take Trail No. 729 out of the parking area for TJ Corral. After 0.25 mile, turn right at the junction, staying on Trail No. 729. Almost immediately, you pass through a gate and into the wilderness. Follow this section of trail as it winds through a brushy desert landscape with views of cliffs in the distance. At mile 2.2, you come to a junction with a trail leading down into Little Bear Canyon. Go straight, staying on Trail No. 729. This canyon is narrow and sometimes the trail leads directly through the creek bed. In a very wet year, or in the event of a flash flood, this would be a terrible place to be. However, in a dry year on a sunny day, it offers stunning scenery. The cliffs rise dramatically on either side, forming amazing shapes. Look carefully to see the couple of small caves and one large cave dotting the cliff walls. The trail is difficult in places, and you may have to get off and lead your horse through tricky areas.

At around mile 4, you come to the junction of Little Bear Canyon and the Middle Fork of the Gila River. A nice flat area among the trees and some good campsites make this a perfect place for an overnight or lunch stop. Take a right onto Trail No. 157 and follow it as it leads alongside the river. The flora here becomes greener and denser. Beautiful patches of thornapple flowers, also known as sacred datura, line the river along with angel trumpets and skyrockets.

Soon you come to the first of almost 30 river crossings. As you make your way across the river, take your time and look for the trail on the other side. It is easy to lose the trail if there is a log to go around or if you are busy keeping branches out of your face and not paying attention. You will be following the river for the next 6 miles. There is no end to adventure along this section of the trail: As soon as you begin to recover from a river crossing or a tangled patch of junglelike greenery, you find yourself faced with another. When we rode this trail, we found a huge rattlesnake blocking our path. It let us know what it thought of our little party with a couple shakes of its massive rattle, and we scurried around it in a wide arc.

About 4.5 miles after reaching the Middle Fork, you come to a trail junction. Stay on Trail No. 157, following the river. The other trail is No. 27, which leads to Whiterocks. Just before mile 9, the trail passes some hot springs alongside the river. You can feel the heat rising out of them as you go by. Right after this, the canyon begins to broaden and a large patch of sunflowers decorates the last part of the trail. At the last river crossing, number 29, a meadow lies off to the right on the other side of the gate. Go to the left, through the river, and up the small hill to the parking area for the visitor center. From here, follow the road 1.25 miles back to the trailhead at TJ Corral.

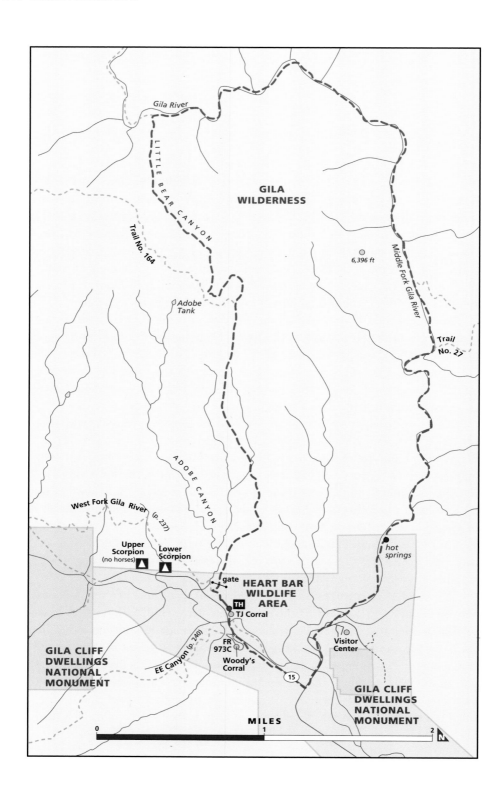

# Iron Creek Mesa

## 76

Gila Wilderness, Gila National Forest,
Wilderness Ranger District

| | |
|---|---|
| 8.25 miles | **Round-Trip Distance** |
| 7,900–8,375 feet | **Elevation Range** |
| Moderate | **Difficulty** |
| May through October | **Best Season** |
| No | **Horse Facilities** |
| Iron Creek Lake, Willow Creek | **Water** |
| Yes | **Shoes Needed** |
| Negrito Mountain USGS 7.5-minute quad | **Maps** |
| Iron Creek Mesa | **Special Attractions** |

## Directions to Trailhead

From Reserve, take NM 435 south out of town. You will pass through San Francisco and Lower San Francisco Plazas before NM 435 enters the Gila National Forest and becomes FR 141 approximately 6 miles from downtown Reserve. About 23 miles from Reserve, the pavement ends and turns into an all-weather gravel road. Continue for an additional 10 miles until reaching the junction with FR 28. Turn right (south) onto FR 28. Follow FR 28 for 12 miles until you reach the intersection for Willow Creek Campground, also signed as FR 507 and CR C073. Turn left (south) onto FR 507. Pass by the entrance to Willow Creek Campground (horses are not allowed in the campground). The trailhead for Trail No. 151 is the next left. There are plenty of areas for trailer parking and dispersed camping at the trailhead.

From Glenwood, take US 180 3.7 miles to the junction with NM 159, which will turn into FR 28. Follow this paved road though Mogollon, where the road will turn into an all-weather gravel road. Continue on this road for just over 27 miles until reaching the turn for FR 507 and CR C073 on your right. This road is winding and narrow and is not open to trailers over 17 feet.

This ride makes a great day trip, taking you across meadows, past lakes, and through a dramatic burn area. If you are interested in camping, keep in mind that horses are not allowed in the campground at Willow Creek. However, you can camp with them at the trailhead on your way into and out of the wilderness. The Forest Service prefers that you not set up a long-term camp at the trailhead.

Trail No. 151 climbs steeply up the hill behind Willow Creek. After riding for about 1.2 miles, you come to Iron Creek Lake and the junction with Trail No. 172. Trail No. 172 takes you up to Whitewater Baldy, a little over 7 miles away. Continue straight across the dam of the shallow and marshy lake. It is rather soupy in the meadow surrounding this little lake, so be cautious if you water your horse here. Continue past the lake as the trail traverses the side of the mountain. In another 0.25 mile, the path intersects with Trail No. 171.

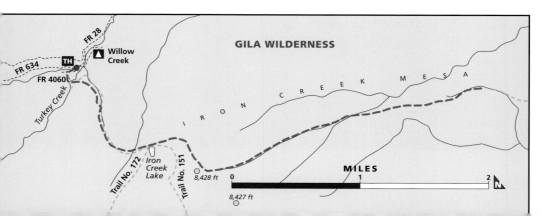

Trail No. 151 continues straight down to Iron Creek, while Trail No. 171 bears left (east) and heads up to Iron Creek Mesa. Turn left and follow No. 171 as it climbs up to the mesa.

A little less than 0.5 mile after turning onto No. 171, you come to a small saddle where all the trees have fallen over. The trail bears left (northeast) and heads down the small drainage. The path is somewhat faint here, and with all the fallen trees, we managed to lose it for a short time. If you lose the trail, just continue down the drainage on the right-hand side and you will pick it back up.

The trail continues to head down the drainage through a beautiful ponderosa pine forest. About 1 mile from the saddle, you arrive at a small meadow. It makes a wonderful place to eat lunch, and our horses enjoyed their lunch here also. At this point, you have traveled just under 3 miles. We continued to ride and soon came to a place recently burned in a forest fire. Most of the ponderosa pine and scrub oak still had their needles or leaves, but they were all brown and dead. Contrasting with the green of the living trees, they made quite an arresting sight.

We continued through the burned area for a while before turning around at approximately mile 4. As you ride through the burned area, watch out for the fire breaks that the firefighters used to stop the fire. Some of them look like the trail, so keep your eyes open. If you have any doubt, follow the trail that heads down the small drainage. A map and compass or GPS would also be helpful.

# 77 Snow Canyon

Gila National Forest, Reserve Ranger District

| | |
|---|---|
| **Round-Trip Distance** | 9.1 miles |
| **Elevation Range** | 8,000–8,250 feet |
| **Difficulty** | Moderate |
| **Best Season** | May through October |
| **Horse Facilities** | Corrals at campground |
| **Water** | Loco Mountain Tank |
| **Shoes Needed** | Yes |
| **Maps** | Loco Mountain USGS 7.5-minute quad |
| **Special Attractions** | Canyons, lush meadows |

## Directions to Trailhead

From Reserve, take NM 435 south out of town. You will pass through San Francisco and Lower San Francisco Plazas before NM 435 enters the Gila National Forest and becomes FR 141 approximately 6 miles from downtown Reserve. About 23 miles from Reserve, the pavement ends and turns into an all-weather gravel road. Continue for an additional 10 miles until reaching the junction with FR 28. Turn right (south) onto FR 28. Follow FR 28 for 9 miles until reaching the junction with FR 142. Turn left (east) onto FR 142, following it for 6 miles until you reach Snow Lake. FR 142 turns left (east), heading toward Aeroplane Mesa Campground 4 miles farther down the road. The road is narrower than the previous gravel roads but is well maintained past the corrals at Aeroplane Mesa Campground. Dipping Vat Campground is next to Snow Lake and has drinking water available. Although horses are not allowed in the campground, areas outside of the campground are available for dispersed camping.

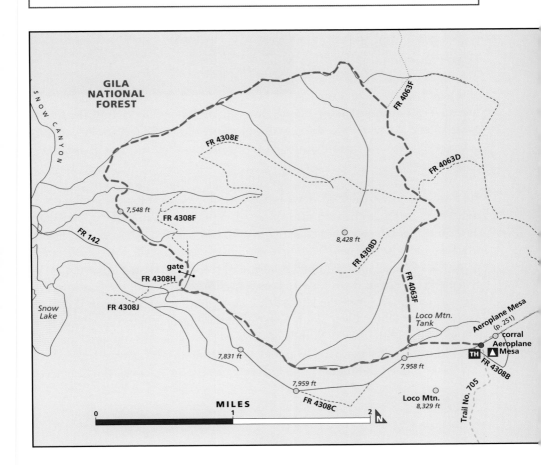

This ride follows a series of old service roads and cattle trails, winding you through beautiful forests at the base of Loco Mountain. From the corrals, head west to Loco Mountain Tank, visible in the distance. After offering your horses water, turn right (north) and head up the two-track road. On maps, it is labeled as FR 4063F, although no signs are posted. Follow this road as it heads uphill. About 1.33 miles from the tank is a four-way intersection, where you should take a right. This road travels downhill slightly and curves into an open meadow. Cross the

meadow toward the shallow mouth of a canyon that heads toward the left (southwest). We rode into the canyon following old cattle trails. The canyon is beautiful, and the healthy, thinned forest surrounding it is full of ancient ponderosa pine.

After traveling through the canyon for about 2 miles, the trail intersects an old Forest Service road with views of Snow Lake. Follow it for 1.25 miles until it intersects with another old road. Here, go right (south) and take this road a short distance to a gate, set across the road to block traffic. The gate was open when we rode the trail, and from here you can continue on the road to the main road (FR 142), go left (east), and follow it all the way back to the corrals.

If you are not ready to leave the canyons, drop down from the gate into the canyon that heads off to the left (east). The beginning of the canyon is rather rocky, with a couple of log and boulder obstacles, but is still manageable. Once you get through the first 0.25 mile of the canyon, it smooths out and you will find old cattle trails and parts of an old road to follow. The canyon leads all the way back to Loco Mountain Tank and you will see the corrals in the distance.

## Directions to Trailhead

From Quemado, travel south on NM 32 for approximately 14.4 miles. Turn left (east) onto NM 103, also called FR 13. The road is paved for 4 miles until reaching Quemado Lake, then turns to all-weather gravel as it passes by four campgrounds. Horses are not allowed in the recreation area surrounding the lake. Continue on FR 13 for 18 miles past the lake until reaching FR 214. Turn left (north) and travel for 1 mile until reaching Valle Tio Vinces Campground and the public corrals on your left.

From Datil, travel approximately 34 miles west on NM 12 until reaching the intersection with FR 214 (also called CR A095) on your right (north). Turn onto FR 214 and travel approximately 9.5 miles until reaching Valle Tio Vinces Campground and the public corrals on your left.

Although there is no water at the corrals, Valle Tio Vinces Spring is just across FR 214 and slightly to the north. When we were in the area in early August, this spring was running well. Be sure to check with the Forest Service for local water conditions.

If you are looking to have a trail to yourself, this ride is a good bet, offering beautiful scenery and a minimum of company. Take the trail heading west out of the back of the campground. We followed it less than 0.25 mile before turning left onto another old road. The road heads sharply to the left and is a little hard to see. Follow it as it curves around the ridge. In less than 0.5 mile, it intersects another forest road. Take this sharp right and head uphill (west) on this road until it eventually peters out. Continue to head uphill, angling slightly toward your left. When you reach the top of the ridge, you'll encounter another forest road, which follows the ridgeline. Go left on this road as it runs parallel to FR 13.

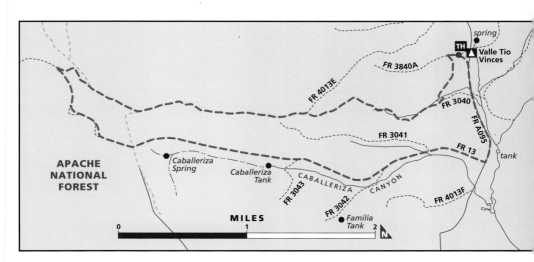

We remained on this road, passing by a couple of other faint roads that lead off to the right. After a total of 4.25 miles, the path intersects with a road heading to the right, more defined and better maintained than the previous ones you have passed. At this point, go left up and over the ridge, away from the defined road and the trail. You will come to FR 13. Take a left and follow it east almost 4 miles back to FR 214, then go left again and ride back to the corrals.

This ride is nice because there is almost no chance of seeing other people and it allows you to choose your path as you go. We knew from the GPS that FR 13 was running parallel to our route and were able to navigate our way back to the corrals with no problem. However, it would not be a good idea to attempt this ride without a GPS or a map and compass.

# Mangas Lookout Tower

**80**

Apache National Forest administered by
Gila National Forest, Quemado Ranger District

| | |
|---|---|
| 10.5 miles | **Round-Trip Distance** |
| 8,100–9,700 feet | **Elevation Range** |
| Moderate | **Difficulty** |
| May through October | **Best Season** |
| Corrals at campground | **Horse Facilities** |
| Valle Tio Vinces Spring | **Water** |
| Yes | **Shoes Needed** |
| Mangas Mountain USGS 7.5-minute quad | **Maps** |
| Outstanding views | **Special Attractions** |

## Directions to Trailhead

Follow the directions to Valle Tio Vinces Campground (ride 79, p. 254).

This ride takes you up a well-maintained forest service road to a fire look-out tower where you are greeted with spectacular views in all directions. Most of the ride is part of the Continental Divide Trail (CDT), traveling a well-graveled road that could be hard on some horses' hooves. Begin from the corrals at the campground and cross FR 214. FR 11 is just north of the corrals by the spring. Head east on FR 11 for approximately 4.3 miles until you come to FR 322, which bears left (east) away from FR 11. The CDT follows FR 322.

Instead of turning onto FR 322, continue to follow FR 11 as it swings south and then back north on its way to the tower. Take your time and enjoy the views from the lookout, but please be respectful of the cabin and tower. We returned by the same route, although an old road is clearly visible from the cabin site and you could try to follow it back to FR 11 to cut some mileage off the return trip.

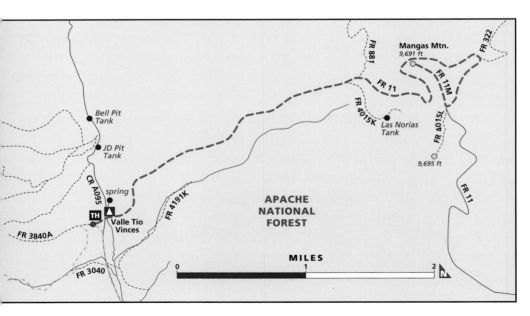

# Sawmill Canyon

## 81

Apache National Forest administered by
Gila National Forest, Quemado Ranger District

| | |
|---:|:---|
| 7 miles | **Round-Trip Distance** |
| 7,800–8,000 feet | **Elevation Range** |
| Easy | **Difficulty** |
| May through October | **Best Season** |
| None | **Horse Facilities** |
| Armijo Spring, small tanks along Sawmill Canyon (may be dry) | **Water** |
| No | **Shoes Needed** |
| Gallo Mountains East USGS 7.5-minute quad | **Maps** |
| Easy canyon ride, ponderosa forest | **Special Attractions** |

## Directions to Trailhead

From Quemado, head south on NM 32 for approximately 18 miles. Turn left (east) onto CR A021. The intersection is marked only by a sign, not by the name of the road. Follow CR A021 for 3.3 miles. It passes through private property, so please be respectful. CR A021 ends at the boundary of the national forest. Turn right for Armijo Campground, go straight for Armijo Spring, and bear left to enter the national forest on FR 854. Horses are not allowed in the actual campground, but there are a number of good areas to highline them or to put up an electric fence. Please remember to camp at least 300 feet from the spring.

This ride stays on forest roads as it meanders among ponderosa pine forests and through Sawmill Canyon. From the campground, take FR 854 east. Stay on FR 854 for 2 miles until it meets Sawmill Canyon on your left. Turn left (north) and follow the former path of FR 13A as it travels down Sawmill Canyon. The road threads through the canyon and is surrounded on both sides by ponderosa pine forest. We rode for about 3.5 miles before deciding to turn around at the point where FR 13A intersects another road heading to the right.

If you want to extend your ride, you have numerous options at this point. This road looks promising, or you could explore the forest road that branches off to the left about 0.33 mile before the turnaround point. The map shows it heading up a small drainage and eventually looping back around to FR 854 just west of Sawmill Canyon. Or you could simply continue to ride down Sawmill Canyon. In a little over 0.8 mile, the road enters private property. Please be respectful and do not trespass. Just before reaching the private property, another forest road branches off to the right. You could follow it back to FR 854 as well. Whatever you decide, it would be a good idea to bring a map and compass or a GPS unit if you plan on exploring one or more of the side roads.

# Armijo Spring

## Apache National Forest administered by Gila National Forest, Quemado Ranger District

| | |
|---|---|
| 9 miles | **Round-Trip Distance** |
| 7,800–8,700 feet | **Elevation Range** |
| Moderate | **Difficulty** |
| May through October | **Best Season** |
| None | **Horse Facilities** |
| Armijo Spring | **Water** |
| Yes | **Shoes Needed** |
| Gallo Mountains East USGS 7.5-minute quad | **Maps** |
| A beautiful ponderosa forest | **Special Attractions** |

## Directions to Trailhead

Follow the directions to Armijo Campground (ride 81, p. 259).

This relaxing 9-mile ride travels along FR 854, a lovely, sandy road perfect for an easy horseback ride through the woods. Keep in mind, though, that it is probably treacherous in a vehicle after a storm. After 1.6 miles heading east and south on FR 854, you'll pass Porcupine Spring (which was dry when we rode) and pass through a gate. In less than 0.5 mile, Sawmill Canyon heads north on your left. The turnoff is marked by a sign, as well as a couple of beautiful old cottonwood trees. We passed the canyon and continued on FR 854.

Two and a half miles from the campground, the road begins to climb. After a couple of switchbacks, it levels out again, passing through a gate at mile 3.9. For the next 0.5 mile, the road leads you through a healthy ponderosa forest before meeting FR 93. This is a good point to turn around, though if you want to extend your trip, you could head east on FR 93 a short distance to FR 043, which goes north to El Caso Lookout. This would be a fairly long ride, so if you are interested in doing it, make sure you start early so you can beat the storms. Be sure also to check with the rangers for current road conditions. The numerous side roads heading off of FR 854 should make interesting exploring, too. There are many small pieces of private land scattered throughout this part of the Gila, however, so please be careful and respect these properties.

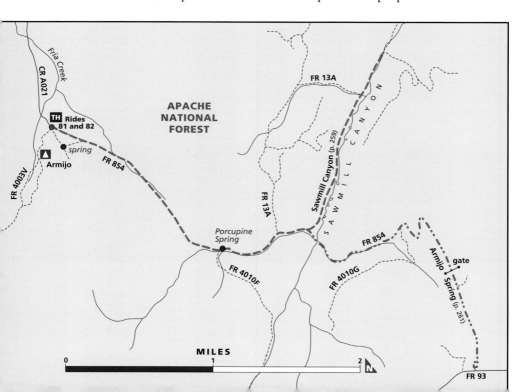

# Appendix: Public Agency Contact Information

## CARSON NATIONAL FOREST
Supervisor's Office, Forest Service Building, 208 Cruz Alta Rd., Taos, NM 87571
(505) 758-6200 • www.fs.fed.us/r3/carson

### Ranger Stations

Camino Real Ranger District
P.O. Box 68
Peñasco, NM 87553
(505) 587-2255

El Rito Ranger District
P.O. Box 56
El Rito, NM 87530
(505) 581-4554

Questa Ranger District
P.O. Box 110
Questa, NM 87556
(505) 586-0520

Canjilon Ranger District
P.O. Box 469
Canjilon, NM 87515
(505) 684-2489

Jicarilla Ranger District
664 E. Broadway
Bloomfield, NM 87413
(505) 632-2956

Tres Piedras Ranger District
P.O. Box 38
Tres Piedras, NM 87577
(505) 758-8678

## CIBOLA NATIONAL FOREST
Supervisor's Office, 2113 Osuna Rd. NE, Ste. A, Albuquerque, NM 87113
(505) 346-3900 • www.fs.fed.us/r3/cibola

### Ranger Stations

Magdalena Ranger District
P.O. Box 45
Magdalena, NM 87825
(505) 854-2281

Mt. Taylor Ranger District
1800 Lobo Canyon Rd.
Grants, NM 87020
(505) 287-8833

Kiowa and Rita Blanca
National Grasslands
714 Main St.
Clayton, NM 88415
(505) 374-9652

Mountainair Ranger District
#40 Ranger Station Rd.
P.O. Box 69
Mountainair, NM 87036
(505) 847-2990

Sandia Ranger District
11776 Hwy. 337
Tijeras, NM 87059
(505) 281-3304

### Visitor Center and Information
Northwest New Mexico Visitor Center
1900 E. Santa Fe Ave.
Grants, NM 87020
(505) 876-2783
www.nps.gov/elma/nnmvc.htm

# GILA NATIONAL FOREST
Supervisor's Office, 3005 E. Camino del Bosque, Silver City, NM 88061
(505) 388-8201 • www.fs.fed.us/r3/gila

## Ranger Stations

Black Range Ranger District
1804 N. Date St.
Truth or Consequences, NM 87901
(505) 894-6677

Glenwood Ranger District
P.O. Box 8
Glenwood, NM 88039
(505) 539-2481

Quemado Ranger District
P.O. Box 159
Quemado, NM 87829
(505) 773-4678

Reserve Ranger District
P.O. Box 170
Reserve, NM 87830
(505) 533-6232

Silver City Ranger District
3005 E. Camino del Bosque
Silver City, NM 88061
(505) 388-8201

Wilderness Ranger District
HC 68 P.O. Box 50
Mimbres, NM 88049
(505) 536-2250

## Visitor Centers and Information

Gila Cliff Dwellings National Monument
  and Gila Visitor Center
Route 11, P.O. Box 100
Silver City, NM 88061
(505) 536-9461
www.nps.gov/gicl/

Luna Work Center
P.O. Box 91
Luna, NM 87824
(505) 547-2611

---

# LINCOLN NATIONAL FOREST
Supervisor's Office, 1101 New York Ave., Alamogordo, NM 88310
(505) 434-7200 • www.fs.fed.us/r3/lincoln

## Ranger Stations

Guadalupe Ranger District
Federal Bldg., Rm. 159
Carlsbad, NM 88220
(505) 885-4181

Sacramento Ranger District
P.O. Box 288
Cloudcroft, NM 88317
(505) 682-2551

Smokey Bear Ranger District
901 Mechem Dr.
Ruidoso, NM 88345
(505) 257-4095

---

# SANTA FE NATIONAL FOREST
Supervisor's Office, 1474 Rodeo Rd., P.O. Box 1689, Santa Fe, NM 87504
(505) 438-7840 • www.fs.fed.us/r3/sfe

## Ranger Stations

Coyote Ranger District
HC 78 Box 1
Coyote, NM 87012
(505) 638-5526

Cuba Ranger District
P.O. Box 130
Cuba, NM 87013
(505) 289-3264

Española Ranger District
1710 N. Riverside Dr.
P.O. Box 3307
Española, NM 87532
(505) 753-7331

Los Alamos Satellite Office
475 20th St.
Los Alamos, NM 87544
(505) 667-5120

Jemez Ranger District
P.O. Box 150
Jemez Springs, NM 87025
(505) 829-3535

Las Vegas Ranger District
1926 N. 7th St.
Las Vegas, NM 87701
(505) 425-3534

Pecos Ranger District
P.O. Drawer 429
Pecos, NM 87552
(505) 757-6121

### Visitor Center and Information

Walatowa Visitor Center
P.O. Box 100
Jemez Pueblo, NM 87024
(505) 834-7235
www.jemezpueblo.org/

## NEW MEXICO STATE PARKS
Energy, Minerals, and Natural Resources Dept.
2040 S. Pacheco, P.O. Box 1147, Santa Fe, NM 87505
(505) 827-7173 • (888) NM-PARKS • www.emnrd.state.nm.us/nmparks/

| | |
|---|---|
| Bluewater Lake State Park | Santa Rosa Lake State Park |
| Lake Route, Box 3419 | P.O. Box 384 |
| Prewitt, NM 87045 | Santa Rosa, NM 88433 |
| (505) 876-2391 | (505) 472-3110 |
| | |
| Cimarron Canyon/ | Sugarite Canyon State Park |
| Eagle Nest Lake State Park | HCR 63 Box 386 |
| P.O. Box 185 | Raton, NM 87740 |
| Eagle Nest, NM 87718 | (505) 445-5607 |
| (505) 377-6271 | |

## BUREAU OF LAND MANAGEMENT
New Mexico State Office, 1474 Rodeo Rd., P.O. Box 27115, Santa Fe, NM 87502
(505) 438-7400 • www.nm.blm.gov

| Carlsbad Field Office | Taos Field Office | **Visitor Center and Information** |
|---|---|---|
| 620 E. Green St. | 226 Cruz Alta Rd. | Wild Rivers Visitor Center |
| Carlsbad, NM 88220 | Taos, NM 87571 | 1120 Cerro Rd. |
| (505) 234-5972 | (505) 758-8851 | Questa, NM 87556 |
| | | (505) 770-1600 |

## NEW MEXICO DEPARTMENT OF GAME AND FISH
Main Office, One Wildlife Way, P.O. Box 25112, Santa Fe, NM 87504
(505) 476-8000 • www.wildlife.state.nm.us

| Albuquerque Office | Raton Office |
|---|---|
| 3841 Midway Pl. NE | 215 York Canyon Rd. |
| Albuquerque, NM 87109 | Raton, NM 87740 |
| (505) 222-4700 | (505) 445-2311 |

## NEW MEXICO TOURISM DEPARTMENT
Lamy Building, 491 Old Santa Fe Trail, Santa Fe, NM 87503
(505) 827-7400 • (800) 545-2070 • www.newmexico.org

# Index

**Note:** Citations followed by the letter "m" denote maps; those followed by the letter "p" denote photos.

## A

Aeroplane Mesa Campground, 236
Aeroplane Mesa ride, 251–253, 253m
Agua Piedra Campground, 31
Agua Piedra ride, 130m, 131–133
Albuquerque Trail ride, 196–198, 198m
Apache National Forest, 254, 257, 259, 261
Argentina Peak ride, 212m, 213–214
Armijo Spring Campground, 236
Armijo Spring ride, 261–263, 262m
Aspen Basin Campground, 147
Aspen Canyon–Big Bonito ride, 212m, 215–216

## B

Baldy Mountain, 59
Barker–Middle Ponil Creek ride, 50–51, 53m
Beatty's Flats ride, 157m, 158–159
Big Bonito–Aspen Canyon ride, 212m, 215–216
Big Canyon, 208p
Big Canyon ride, 228m, 229–230
Big Costilla Peak, 76
black bear, 22p
Bluewater Lake ride, 188–189, 189m
Bluewater Lake State Park
  description of, 184
  rides in, 188
Bluff Springs–Willie White Canyon ride, 217–219, 219m

Bonita Canyon ride, 52–53, 53m
Borrego Mesa Campground, 147
Bosque–Cerro Blanco ride, 198m, 199–200
Brazos Outlook ride, 112–114, 114m
Bull-of-the-Woods Pasture ride, 93–95, 95m

## C

Cabresto Lake, 85, 87
Cabresto Lake ride, 85–86, 89m
Caja del Rio Canyon, 168
camping ethics/etiquette, 18–19
Camp Wilderness Ridge, 206p
Camp Wilderness Ridge ride, 226–228, 228m
Cañoncito–Cienega ride, 190–192, 192m
Carson National Forest, 85, 90, 93, 110, 123, 126, 128, 131
Cave Creek ride, 160–162, 161m
Cerro Blanco–Bosque ride, 198m, 199–200
Chamas Valley, 120
Cibola National Forest, 185
Cienega–Cañoncito ride, 190–192, 192m
Cimarron Campground, 28
Cimarron Canyon State Park
  description of, 32–33
  rides in, 40, 43
Clayton Corrals–Valle Vidal ride, 71–72, 72m
climate, 12, 23–24
clothing, 16
Columbine Creek ride, 90–92, 92m
Columbine-Hondo Wilderness Study Area, 96

Crest Trail, 190

Cruces Basin Wilderness
   description of, 29–31
   rides in, 107, 115
   views of, 112

**D**

dehydration, 24

Diablo Creek ride, 115–117, 117m

difficulty ratings, 11

Dipping Vat Campground, 236

distances, 11

**E**

Eagle Nest Lake, 40, 43

Eagle Nest Lake ride, 45–47, 47m

Eagle Nest Lake State Park
   description of, 32–33
   rides in, 45

Edward Sargent State Wildlife Area
   description of, 33
   rides in, 118, 120

EE Canyon, 20p

EE Canyon ride, 238m, 240–241

elevations, 11

Elliot Barker State Wildlife Area
   description of, 33
   rides in, 48, 50, 52

El Malpais National Monument, 210, 213

equipment, 16–17

Escondido Creek ride, 107–109, 109m

ethics/etiquette, camping and trail, 18–19

**F**

first aid kits, 25

Fourth of July Campground, 184

FR 306 ride, 153–154, 154m

**G**

gear, 16–17

Gila National Forest, 248

Gila River, 251

Gila Wilderness
   description of, 235–236
   rides in, 237, 240, 242, 245, 251
   views of, 240

Gold Hill ride, 95m, 96–97

Green Mountain ride, 43–44, 44m

Guadalupe Ranger District, description of, 208

**H**

Heart Lake ride, 87–89, 89m

Hopewell Lake
   description of, 29–31
   views of, 126

Hopewell Lake Campground, 30

Hopewell Lake ride, 123–125, 125m

Horseshoe Lake ride, 79–81, 84m

horseshoes, 13

**I**

Iron Creek Mesa ride, 245–247, 246m

Iron Gate Campground, 147

**J**

Jacks Creek Campground, 147–148

Jawbone Mountain ride, 125m, 126–127

**K**

Knob ride, The, 128–130, 130m

# L

La Belle ride, 73–75, 75m

La Cueva Non-Motorized Trail System, description of, 209

Lagunitas Creek ride, 109m, 110–111

Lake Alice Campground, 32

Lake Maloya Trail ride, 36m, 38–39

Las Lagunitas Campground, 30–31

Latir Peak Wilderness
  description of, 29
  rides in, 87

lightning, 23–24

Lincoln National Forest, 217, 220, 223, 226, 229, 231

Little Bear Canyon, 242

Little Costilla Peak, 59, 76

Lonesome Ridge ride, 228m, 231–233

Long Canyon, 96

Los Taños Equestrian Trail ride, 170–171, 171m

# M

Mangas Lookout Tower ride, 257–258, 258m

Manzano Mountain Wilderness
  description of, 183–184
  rides in, 196, 199, 201, 204

maps
  key to symbols, 6
  obtaining and using, 10
  statewide, 6m–7m

Maverick Campground, 32–33

McCrystal Campground, 28

McCrystal Place ride, 59–61, 60m

Middle Fork Gila River ride, 242–244, 244m

Middle Fork Rio Santa Barbara ride, 134–136, 136m

Middle Ponil Creek–Barker ride, 50–51, 53m

Middle Ponil Creek ride, 68–70, 69m

Moreno Valley, 40, 43

Mount Taylor ride, 185–187, 186m

Mt. Taylor Ranger District, description of, 182–183

# N

Nabor Lake ride, 118–119, 122m

Nambe Lake ride, 165–167, 166m

North Ponil Creek ride, 54–56, 56m

# O

Opportunity Trail ride, 35–37, 36m

Ox Canyon ride, 203m, 204–205

# P

Pecos Baldy Lake, 145p

Pecos Baldy Lake ride, 155–157, 157m

Pecos River, 158

Pecos Wilderness
  description of, 31, 147–148
  rides in, 134, 137, 140, 143, 149, 151, 155, 158, 160, 163, 165

Philmont Baldy, 26p

Ponderosa Campground, 32–33

Ponil Complex Fire of 2002, 50, 52, 68

Ponil Park, 54, 62

Porcupine Canyon, 251

Powderhouse Canyon ride, 76–78, 77m

# Q

Quemado Ranger District, description of, 236

# R

Red Canyon Campground, 183
Red Canyon ride, 201–203, 203m
Reilly Ranch, 170, 172
Resumidero Campground, 148
Ridge Ride ride, 120–122, 122m
Rim Trail ride, 220–222, 221m
Rim Trail–Sunspot ride, 223–225, 224m
Ring Ranch, 62
Ring Ranch ride, 57–58, 58m
Rio de las Vacas ride, 177–178, 178m
Rio de los Pinos Campground, 30–31
Rio Grande Gorge ride, 104–106, 105m
Rio Grande ride, 168–169, 169m
Rio Grande, 104, 168
Rio Grande Valley, 199, 201, 204
Rio Grande Wild and Scenic River
  Recreation Area
    description of, 34
    rides in, 104
Rio Medio ride, 149–150, 154m
Rio Quemado ride, 151–152, 154m

# S

Sacramento Ranger District, description of, 207
safety
  avoiding getting lost, 21–22
  avoiding losing your horse, 21
  first aid kits, 25
  on the trail, 20–21
  respecting wildlife, 22–23
  summer storms and lightning, 23–24
  warm weather and dehydration, 12–13, 24

Salitre Tank ride, 171m, 172–173
Sandia Mountain Wilderness
  description of, 183
  rides in, 190, 193
San Gregorio Reservoir ride, 174–176, 176m
San Leonardo Lakes ride, 140–142, 142m
San Pedro Parks ride, 179–181, 180m
San Pedro Parks Wilderness
  description of, 148
  rides in, 174, 177, 179
Santa Barbara Campground, 31
Santa Fe Baldy, 163
Santa Fe National Forest, 153, 168
Santa Rosa Lake State Park, 170, 172
Sawmill Canyon, 234p
Sawmill Canyon ride, 259–260, 262m
Sawmill Park ride, 82–84, 84m
Scorpion Campground, 235
Seally Canyon ride, 62–64, 64m
seasons, 12, 23–24
shoes (horse), 13
Shuree Lodge, 65
Shuree Ponds ride, 65–67, 66m
Snow Canyon ride, 248–250, 249m
Soda Pocket Campground, 32
South Crest Trail ride, 193–195, 194m
Southfork Campground, 207
Spirit Lake ride, 163–164, 166m
Sugarite Canyon State Park
  description of, 32
  rides in, 35, 38
summer storms and lightning, 23–24
Sunspot–Rim Trail ride, 223–225, 224m

## T

Taylor, Mount, 182p, 185
Tolby Campground, 32–33
Tolby Meadow ride, 40–42, 41m
Touch-Me-Not Mountain, 43
trail ethics/etiquette, 18–19
Trampas Lake, 12p
Trampas Lakes ride, 142m, 143–145
trip planning/preparation
  best seasons, 12
  clothing, 16
  equipment, 16–17
  getting in riding shape, 14
  obtaining and using maps, 10
  traveling with your horse, 14–15
  water availability, 12–13, 24
Tularosa Basin, 210, 213, 220, 223
Turkey Canyon ride, 210–212, 212m
Twining Campground, 29

## V

Valle Tio Vinces Campground, 236
Valle Tio Vinces ride, 254–256, 255m
Valle Vidal
  description of, 27–28
  rides in, 54, 57, 59, 62, 65, 68, 71, 73, 76
Valle Vidal–Clayton Corrals ride, 71–72, 72m
Vidal Creek, 71

## W

water, 12–13, 24
weather, 12, 23–24
West Fork Gila River ride, 237–239, 238m
West Fork Rio Santa Barbara ride, 136m, 137–139
Wheeler Peak, 40
Wheeler Peak ride, 98–101, 101m
Wheeler Peak Wilderness
  description of, 28–29
  rides in, 79, 82, 98, 102
White Mountain Wilderness
  description of, 206–207
  rides in, 210, 213, 215
White Sands, 210
wilderness areas, traveling in, 13
wildlife, 22–23
Williams Lake ride, 101m, 102–103
Willie White Canyon–Bluff Springs ride, 217–219, 219m
Willow Creek Campground, 235
Wilson Mesa, 26p
Wilson Mesa ride, 48–49, 53m

## About the Authors/Photographers

**Nina Buonaiuto-Cloyed** grew up in Santa Fe, New Mexico. She graduated from the University of New Mexico in 2003 with a degree in University Studies. She currently works in Santa Fe as an elementary school teacher.

**John Buonaiuto-Cloyed** grew up with horses in Riverside, Iowa. He attended Iowa Wesleyan College and graduated with a degree in Physical Education. They met high in an alpine meadow at the Philmont Boy Scout Ranch while employed there for the summer. John taught Nina the joys of riding. This is their first book.

Nina and John were accompanied on these rides by their four horses, Cuervo and Beamer—full brothers born in Riverside, Iowa—and Brownie and Cougar, who both proved to be champs during a full summer of trail riding. This book is in memory of Brownie: It was his last great adventure before reaching that greener pasture in the sky. We miss you, bud.